AS/A-LEVEL YEAR 1

STUDENT GUIDE

OCR

Economics

Macroeconomics 1

Sam Dobin

PHILIP ALLAN FOR
HODDER
EDUCATION
AN HACHETTE UK COMPANY

Philip Allan, an imprint of Hodder Education, an Hachette UK company, Blenheim Court, George Street, Banbury, Oxfordshire OX16 5BH

Orders

Bookpoint Ltd, 130 Milton Park, Abingdon, Oxfordshire OX14 4SB

tel: 01235 827827

fax: 01235 400401

e-mail: education@bookpoint.co.uk

Lines are open 9.00 a.m.–5.00 p.m., Monday to Saturday, with a 24-hour message answering service. You can also order through the Hodder Education website: www.hoddereducation.co.uk

© Sam Dobin 2015

ISBN 978-1-4718-4426-3

First printed 2015

Impression number 5 4 3 2

Year 2019 2018 2017 2016

This Guide has been written specifically to support students preparing for the OCR AS and A-level Economics examinations. The content has been neither approved nor endorsed by OCR and remains the sole responsibility of the author.

Typeset by Integra Software Services Pvt. Ltd., Pondicherry, India

Cover photo: Iakov Kalinin/Fotolia

Printed in Italy

Hachette UK's policy is to use papers that are natural, renewable and recyclable products and made from wood grown in sustainable forests. The logging and manufacturing processes are expected to conform to the environmental regulations of the country of origin.

Contents

■ Getting the most from this book

Exam tips

Advice on key points in the text to help you learn and recall content, avoid pitfalls, and polish your exam technique in order to boost your grade.

Knowledge check

Rapid-fire questions throughout the Content Guidance section to check your understanding.

Knowledge check answers

1 Turn to the back of the book for the Knowledge check answers.

Summaries

■ Each core topic is rounded off by a bullet-list summary for quick-check reference of what you need to know.

Exam-style questions

Commentary on the questions

Tips on what you need to do to gain full marks, indicated by the icon **e**

Sample student answers

Practise the questions, then look at the student answers that follow.

Commentary on sample student answers

Find out how many marks each answer would be awarded in the exam and then read the comments (preceded by the icon **e**) following each student answer. Annotations that link back to points made in the student answers show exactly how and where marks are gained or lost.

Questions & Answers

(d) Using Figure 2, explain whether it is true to say that Estonia's balance of trade in goods and services went from a deficit to a surplus between 2008 and 2010. [3 marks]

e Begin by stating whether the statement is true or false. If it is true, use data to explain why. If it is not true, you need to provide the correct explanation of what happened to Estonia's balance of trade and offer evidence to support this explanation.

(e) 'In 1994, Estonia became the first country in Europe to adopt a flat tax rate on income tax.'

Evaluate whether adopting a flat tax rate represents a good system of taxation. [8 marks]

e The directive word 'Evaluate' means a two-sided answer is required here. You should begin by analysing why a flat tax rate system may represent a good system of taxation, using any features of a 'good' tax which apply here. This should be followed by a consideration of any of the features of a 'good' tax which a flat tax system does not offer. Finally, a judgement needs to be offered in which you reach a conclusion over whether the advantages of a flat tax system outweigh the disadvantages, supporting this conclusion with an explanation of why you have come to this decision.

(f) Evaluate the extent to which imbalances on the balance of payments are harmful to an economy. [12 marks]

e The directive word 'Evaluate' means a two-sided answer is required here. Begin by offering detailed economic analysis of why imbalances may harm an economy, remembering to refer to the macroeconomic policy objectives. Then consider circumstances in which imbalances would not be particularly harmful, supporting these points with a thorough explanation. Finally reach a supported judgement which justifies whether imbalances on the balance of payments are harmful to an economy.

Student A

(a) The size of the multiplier can be calculated by 1 ÷ marginal propensity to withdraw.

MPW = 0.2 + 0.3 + 0.1 = 0.6

Multiplier = 1 ÷ 0.6 = 1.67

So a €55 million tax cut should result in an increase in output of:

55 million × 1.67 = **€91.85 million**

e 3/3 marks awarded. Candidate correctly calculates the multiplier effect. However, they should have stated the equation for the marginal propensity to withdraw so the examiner could have awarded marks for their workings if they had made a mistake with the calculation. The multiplier is then correctly applied to calculate the impact on national income of the tax cut.

70 OCR Economics

■ About this book

This guide is designed to prepare you for the AS and A-level OCR macroeconomics exams. The guide covers all of the content required to sit the AS exam and approximately half of the content required to sit the A-level exam. It includes sample questions and answers to prepare you for both papers.

The guide is split into two sections:

Content Guidance

This section details the core macroeconomic themes and models you need to understand to excel in this course:

- Economic policy objectives and indicators of macroeconomic performance
- Aggregate demand and aggregate supply
- The application of policy instruments
- The global context

You should make sure you have fully mastered all of the content in this guide before progressing onto the practice questions. Use the knowledge checks as you work through the guide to test your understanding and take on board the exam tips to avoid falling into the traps that most commonly result in students losing marks. At the end of each topic area there is a bullet-pointed summary of the content covered – if you are unable to offer a detailed explanation of any part of this, you should read the section again to clear up any misunderstanding.

Questions & Answers

This section begins by setting out the format of the AS and A-level OCR macroeconomics exam papers. It gives you advice on how long to spend on each question and offers important tips on how to maximise your marks on the different elements of the paper. It also explains the levels system used to mark essays.

This is followed by a series of sample questions, covering all the different types of assessment seen in both the AS and A-level papers – multiple-choice, data response and essays. After all these questions there are some example answers from students. You should practise all these questions yourself and compare your answers to the example answers while reading the detailed exam advice to improve your understanding of what is required to achieve full marks.

Content Guidance

■ Economic policy objectives and indicators of macroeconomic performance

Economic growth

Economic growth represents an increase in the total output produced by an economy. It is often considered to be the most important macroeconomic policy objective because an increase in output essentially means there are more goods and services available for consumers to enjoy, therefore raising individuals' material standard of living. In developing countries, where poverty often exists because of a scarcity of resources, increasing the availability of resources (which economic growth achieves) is clearly crucial.

The government targets **sustainable economic growth**. This is important because a one-off period of growth which is not sustained over time, or growth which occurs by using up finite non-renewable resources and therefore results in reduced potential output in the future, is not desirable as it will not lead to the long-term improvements in standard of living targeted by the policy objective. There is clearly a trade-off between rapid economic growth today and growth in the future; the sustainability element of the objective attempts to address this conflict.

It is important to understand the difference between short-run and long-run economic growth:

- *Short-run economic growth* – an increase in actual output produced in an economy. In Figure 1, this can be illustrated by the movement from production point A to production point B, where existing factors of production are used more fully or efficiently to increase the level of output.
- *Long-run economic growth* – an increase in potential output. In Figure 1, this can be illustrated by a shift in the production possibility curve from PPC_0 to PPC_1. It does not mean that more output has actually been produced but means there is the potential for output to increase in the future as a result of an increase in the economy's productive capacity.

Measuring economic growth

Economic growth is calculated by measuring the percentage change in gross domestic product (GDP) in the economy per annum. It is important to understand the difference between real and nominal GDP growth. Change in real GDP is a more accurate measure of economic growth because it accounts for the effects of inflation – any increase in nominal GDP does not necessarily suggest that output has

> **Sustainable economic growth** An increase in output today which does not harm the ability of future generations to increase the output of the economy in the future.

> **Knowledge check 1**
>
> Explain how Figure 1 could be used to illustrate short-run and long-run economic growth occurring simultaneously.

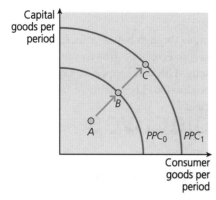

Figure 1 Capital and consumer goods per period

increased, as it may simply be the case that rising prices have increased the value of that output. For example, nominal GDP growth of 2.4% at a time when the rate of inflation was 2% would suggest that real GDP has increased by only 0.4%.

GDP is a desirable method of measuring economic growth because it is easy to interpret and relatively straightforward to calculate, allowing for comparisons between countries to be made. It provides a very clear indication about the material standard of living in a country. However, there are a number of difficulties involved in measuring economic growth which it is important to be aware of:

■ *Population differences* – GDP does not take into account the dramatic differences which exist between the populations of countries. Just because China's GDP is higher than the UK's does not mean Chinese citizens have a higher material standard of living – their population is more than 20 times bigger!

■ *Inequality* – GDP measures the total output produced in an economy but gives no sense of how this is distributed; standard of living may on average be higher in a country with lower GDP but a more equal distribution of income.

■ *Informal economic activity* – much output that is produced is non-marketed (such as production which takes place within households for their own consumption). In some countries there is also a large black market, where illegal production and exchange accounts for a large volume of economic activity. In countries where there is a significant amount of informal economic activity, GDP is likely to underestimate total output.

■ *Social indicators* – economic growth cannot alone be used to measure standard of living because there are many other factors which affect individuals' well-being, such as their access to education and healthcare. In fact, in some instances economic growth can cause direct harm to well-being, such as production that takes place which harms the environment.

One way to account for differences in population is to use GDP per capita to measure economic growth. This can be calculated by:

GDP per capita = Real GDP ÷ Population

This gives a more accurate indication of standard of living within a country and enables comparisons to be made between countries which have different populations.

Exam tip

A developing country's economic growth rate could be overestimated because as countries develop, economic activity moves from the informal to the formal sector. Therefore, some of the 'increase' in output may not really represent increased output – much of the output may have been produced before but not have been recorded.

Causes of economic growth

In the short run, economic growth can be achieved simply through better or increased utilisation of existing factors of production. In the long run, economic growth can be achieved by expanding the economy's productive capacity. This can happen as a result of an increase in the quantity or quality of factors of production. The quality of factors of production is often measured in terms of their efficiency.

The following table summarises how the quantity or efficiency of the factors of production can be increased.

Factor of production	Quantity	Efficiency
Labour	Any factor which causes an increase in the size of the labour force through population growth or increasing participation rates.	Education and training is the primary tool used by governments to improve workers' productivity.
Capital	Investment in capital such as machinery. Note that there is an increase in the quantity of capital only if net investment is positive – if investment is simply replacing the depreciating capital there is no increase in the quantity of capital.	Technological progress means the efficiency of capital is advancing constantly over time.
Land	The discovery of natural resources has been important to the growth of resource-rich economies.	Development in agricultural techniques, such as crop rotation, is a good example of how land can be used more efficiently.
Enterprise	Ensuring there is a strong market incentive increases the amount of entrepreneurship in an economy – many countries transitioning from command to market economies have experienced a significant increase in the quantity of enterprise as a consequence.	Enterprise education is an increasingly important part of the government's education provision in some nations. The government can also incentivise enterprise through supporting small businesses.

Consequences of economic growth

Generally economic growth is considered beneficial to an economy for the following reasons:

- *Increases material standard of living* – rising GDP per capita means individuals are able to afford more goods and services.
- *Reduced unemployment* – more workers are needed to produce the higher level of output, meaning there is a higher derived demand for labour.
- *Improves public services* – the government will receive more tax revenue as firms are making greater profits and individuals are earning higher incomes and spending more. Benefit payments fall because more people are in work. This means the government has more money to spend on providing public services such as health and education.

However, there are some important drawbacks of economic growth which need to be considered when evaluating these benefits:

- *Environmental harms* – if the increase in output generates pollution or causes environmental degradation, it could harm the quality of life of current and future generations.

Knowledge check 3

Give examples of how a country's population and participation rate could increase.

Knowledge check 4

How can economic growth help to reduce poverty?

- *Worsens well-being* — if the increase in output is caused by people working longer hours this could reduce the amount of time people have to consume leisure, which has a negative impact on their well-being.
- *Worsens inequality* — if the wealth generated from increased output benefits only a small section of the population, this can actually increase the gap between rich and poor, worsening the distribution of income and wealth.
- *Increases inflation* — if the economy is growing too quickly and aggregate demand is rising more quickly than aggregate supply, economic growth can generate demand-pull inflation.

Recessions

An economy is in a recession when there is negative GDP growth for two consecutive quarters. The UK experienced a prolonged period of recession in 2008–09, when output fell for five consecutive quarters.

Recessions have the potential to cause significant harm to an economy. Assuming the size of the population is unchanged, falling GDP means GDP per capita is falling, meaning individuals' material standard of living declines because their real incomes are falling. Moreover, because of falling aggregate demand, firms begin to lay off workers, meaning unemployment rises. This puts pressure on the government budget, which is faced with increasing demands for benefits at a time when tax receipts are falling. A budget deficit is therefore inevitable, which will add to the size of government debt. This can become particularly problematic when the government has not been running a budget surplus during times of economic growth; this occurred in the aftermath of the 2008 financial crisis, when concerns arose about the size of the national debt, which was being added to every year because of a large budget deficit.

Exam tip

Remember that an economy is not in recession when the rate of economic growth is falling but when it is negative – i.e. output has to be falling, not just rising at a slower rate.

Employment and unemployment

The number of people employed – either as employees working for firms or organisations or as self-employed individuals working for themselves – stood at approximately 30 million in the UK in 2014.

It is important to understand how different individuals in the population can be categorised. The population is comprised of two groups of individuals:

- *Working age population* – the number of people living in the UK aged between 16 and 64. It is important to note that while an individual aged 65 is not considered part of the working age population because the retirement age still stands at 65, this does not mean that no individuals aged 65 and above are in employment – one of the features of the labour market today is that an increasing number of older workers are participating in the market.
- *Those outside of working age* – this represents children under the age of 16 (most of whom will be in education) and individuals over the age of 65 (most of whom will be retired).

The working age population can then be divided into a further two sub-categories:

- *Economically active* – individuals of working age who are willing and able to work.
- *Economically inactive* – individuals of working age who are not looking for work because they are either not willing or not able to work.

Knowledge check 5

Give examples of groups of individuals who would be classed as being economically inactive.

The number of individuals who are economically active is referred to as the labour force. The labour force is comprised of individuals who are both employed and **unemployed**.

An important macroeconomic objective is to achieve full employment. This occurs when the vast majority of individuals who are economically active are in work – there are few individuals who would like to work who cannot do so. This is clearly vital, as an economy which is not achieving full employment is not utilising all of its factors of production, meaning output will be lower than it could be. It is difficult to put a numerical value on full employment because it is not equal to zero unemployment – this would be an unrealistic target, as realistically there will always be individuals moving between jobs; while these individuals are temporarily unemployed, this is an inevitable outcome of a flexible labour market rather than a sign of resources being wasted.

Reducing the rate of unemployment is always a priority for the government, as it enables output to increase while at the same time improving the government budget by reducing the number of people claiming benefits and increasing tax receipts. It is interesting to see how in recent years an increasing focus has been placed on reducing the rates of economic inactivity by reforming the benefits system and improving the availability of childcare. This is of course another method of achieving economic growth, as when individuals transition from being economically inactive to economically active the size of the labour force increases, expanding the economy's productive capacity.

> **Unemployed** Individuals of working age who are willing and able to work but are unable to find a job.

> **Knowledge check 6**
>
> Which measure of unemployment is likely to give the largest unemployment rate? Why?

Measuring unemployment

There are two measures of unemployment you need to know about for the exam:

	Claimant count	International Labour Organisation (ILO) unemployment rate
Method	Measures the number of individuals in receipt of unemployment benefit (Jobseeker's Allowance). To be eligible, individuals must declare they are out of work and actively seeking work in the week in which the claim is made.	This is measured through the Labour Force Survey, asking individuals whether they are unemployed by seeing whether they are: *without a job, have actively sought work in the last four weeks and are available to start in the next two weeks OR are out of work, have found a job and are waiting to start it in the next two weeks.*
Advantages	This can be measured easily and cheaply as the government already has a record of the number of people claiming unemployment benefit.	It allows for international comparisons as the ILO measure is used across the world. It includes many individuals who are unemployed but are excluded from the claimant count.
Disadvantages	It includes many individuals who claim they are seeking work but in reality are not actually prepared to work. It excludes many individuals who are unemployed but are not eligible to receive benefit or who choose not to claim benefit. This is a particular problem in countries without an established benefits system, where there is no incentive for individuals to 'sign on'.	Because the estimate is arrived at through a survey, it involves extrapolating from a sample of data to give an estimate of the rate of unemployment across the whole country. This means the estimate is unlikely to be wholly accurate.

A trend which has been evident in the UK labour market in recent years is rising underemployment. Individuals are defined as being underemployed when they are in work but not being utilised to their productive capacity. Examples include individuals who are working part time because they are unable to find full-time employment and individuals who are in jobs significantly below their skill level because they cannot find work which more closely matches their qualifications. This group of individuals is of interest to economists as, like the unemployed, it demonstrates potential capacity which is not being utilised. However, such individuals are not accounted for in unemployment data because they are in work.

Causes of unemployment

Unemployment can be categorised into a number of different causes:

- *Frictional unemployment* – at any one time there will be a number of individuals without work because they are between jobs. Job search is rarely instantaneous – when an individual leaves one job they will be engaged in a period of search or will be waiting to start their new job. This type of unemployment is short term and therefore not particularly damaging.

- *Structural unemployment* – over time, the nature of economic activity within an economy changes. Structural unemployment occurs when the skills of workers do not match the needs of firms which are expanding. For example, a number of highly skilled workers in the manufacturing sector experienced structural unemployment in the late 1980s as industrial production was outsourced to low-wage countries; these workers' skills were therefore no longer demanded and these same individuals did not have the skills required by the emerging tertiary-sector firms. Such workers are likely to remain unemployed in the long term unless they are able to train for a different profession.

- *Cyclical unemployment* – because labour is a derived demand which is demanded only for the output it produces, unemployment is likely to be high during times of recession when there is a low level of aggregate demand in the economy, as workers are made redundant by firms cutting back on their production. This is known as demand-deficient unemployment and can be particularly damaging to an economy as it is likely to affect a significant number of workers at the same time.

- *Seasonal unemployment* – workers in some industries are subject to intermittent periods of unemployment because their labour is demanded at certain times of year only. For example, fruit pickers are not needed all year round. This is a particular problem for many developing countries, where a high proportion of workers are often employed in agriculture or tourism.

- *Voluntary unemployment* – there are a number of individuals in the economy who are without work and actively seeking work who have rejected job offers because they are not prepared to work for the wage rate offered. Such individuals are referred to as being voluntarily unemployed, as by rejecting the job offer they are effectively choosing to be out of work.

Consequences of unemployment

Unemployment is generally considered harmful to an economy because it results in the following:

- *Lost output* – the economy is not fully utilising its scarce resources, meaning output is below the productive potential.

- *Worsened standard of living* – the existence of unemployment means there are some individuals who would like to work who instead have to rely on benefits, meaning they can afford to consume fewer goods and services because of their lower real

Knowledge check 7

Why could frictional unemployment be considered beneficial to an economy?

Knowledge check 8

Explain the relationship between the level of unemployment benefits and the number of people who are voluntarily unemployed.

disposable income. Moreover, morale and well-being are likely to be harmed if individuals experience unemployment for an extended period of time.

- *Pressure on government finances* – the government loses tax revenue from individuals who are paying no income tax and paying less indirect tax because of their reduced spending. At the same time the government is supporting these individuals through social security benefits. This could force the government to borrow more, cut spending in other areas or raise taxes to finance this expenditure.

However, the extent to which unemployment is damaging depends upon the following:

- *The cause of unemployment* – a low level of frictional unemployment can actually be beneficial to an economy as it is a sign of a flexible labour market. Structural unemployment, however, could result in long-term harm for the individuals affected.
- *The level of unemployment* – a high rate of unemployment will put more pressure on the government budget than a low rate of unemployment. A moderate amount of unemployment can be desirable because it creates a degree of spare capacity in the economy, helping to reduce demand-side inflationary pressures.
- *The average duration of unemployment* – individuals who experience short periods of unemployment are unlikely to experience a significant decline in their material standard of living, as they will be able to live off income accrued during their time in employment. However, a high average duration of unemployment is likely to result in **hysteresis**, which could permanently reduce the productive capacity of an economy.

Hysteresis A period of unemployment resulting in the deterioration of an individual's skills, which results in them being permanently less attractive to an employer, increasing the probability of them being unemployed in the long term. This becomes more problematic the longer an individual remains out of a paid job.

Inflation

The concept of inflation explains why individuals are not necessarily better off when their wage rate increases. Suppose in 2011 a worker was offered a 3% pay rise. Assuming the price of goods and services was unchanged, this would mean this individual could afford to buy 3% more goods and services than they could afford in 2010. In reality, though, stable prices is an unrealistic assumption. Over time prices tend to increase – this concept is known as **inflation**. In 2011, the rate of inflation in the UK was 4.5%. This means that, in order for an individual to be able to afford the same amount of goods and services in 2011 as they could afford in 2010, their wage would have to be increased by 4.5%. Given their wage has increased by only 3%, we can conclude that their real income has fallen. Understanding the difference between real and nominal values is extremely important in economics – in this instance the individual's nominal income (which does not take into account any changes in prices) has increased by 3% but their real income (which takes into account changes in prices) has fallen by 1.5%.

Inflation A sustained increase in the general level of prices.

The government targets price stability, which since 2003 has been defined as being a rate of inflation of 2%. The responsibility of delivering this target rests with the Bank of England. It is a symmetric target – inflation 1% below target is as undesirable as inflation 1% above target.

Price stability is important because it avoids the uncertainty that can result from significantly fluctuating prices and the harm to international competitiveness that can be caused by a high rate of inflation.

Measuring inflation

The primary method used to measure inflation in the UK is the Consumer Price Index (CPI). This is constructed in the following way:

1   Using a variety of methods to measure consumer behaviour, including family expenditure surveys, a 'basket' of 680 commonly purchased goods and services is constructed.

2   The prices of these goods and services are measured monthly across a range of different outlets and recorded in index form.

3   The items in the basket are weighted according to the proportion of consumer income they account for – for example, if petrol takes up a higher proportion of consumer income than bread, it will be assigned a higher weighting in the index.

4   The percentage change in the index represents the rate of inflation.

Using an index is an effective way of measuring changes in prices as it allows us to compare current values relative to base values, which is particularly useful when comparing price changes of items with very different prices. For example, it is not easy to compare changes in the prices of bread and cars when told that the price of bread has increased from £1.10 to £1.14 and the price of cars has increased from £8,500 to £8,750 between 2014 and 2015. However, when recorded as index numbers, with prices in the base year (2014) set at an index of 100, comparisons can be made more easily:

- Bread 2015 Index = 100 + [(£1.14 – £1.10) ÷ £1.10 × 100] = **103.6**
- Cars 2015 Index = 100 + [(£8,750 – £8,500) ÷ £8,500 × 100] = **102.9**

The higher value on the bread index tells us the price of bread has increased by more than the price of cars (3.6% and 2.9% respectively).

Alternative measures of inflation

For many years, inflation in the UK was measured using the Retail Prices Index (RPI). This is calculated in a similar way to the Consumer Price Index, using a weighted basket of goods and services to measure price changes in the economy, but there are some important differences:

- The RPI excludes pensioner households and the highest income-earning households, whereas the CPI does not.
- The RPI includes mortgage interest payments, which are excluded from the CPI.
- The RPI uses the arithmetic mean whereas the CPI uses the geometric mean.

When the RPI was used as the official measure of inflation in the UK, the target rate of inflation was set according to the RPIX, which removed mortgage interest rates from the measure in the way the CPI does. There is debate over the relative merits of this. Policy makers argue that given interest rates are used to control inflation, it would be misleading to include mortgage interest payments within the measure of inflation. However, others argue that excluding one of the most significant costs to households from the basket weakens the measure as a true indicator of the cost of living.

Regardless of the measure used, the fixed weightings applied to goods and services within the basket harm the accuracy of the measure. This is because it assumes when

Knowledge check 9

Calculate the rate of inflation if the price index increased from 143 to 149.

the price of a particular good or service rises, individuals continue to spend the same proportion of their income on it. In reality, many individuals will switch away from the good or service to a substitute which is not rising in price to the same extent. Ignoring this substitution effect means measures of inflation are often over-stated.

Finally, the inflation rate is not a good indicator of changes in the cost of living for any one individual because all individuals consume different sets of goods and services. The rate of inflation for an individual is therefore likely to differ from the average generated by the basket of goods and services.

Causes of inflation

There are two primary causes of inflation:

- *Demand-pull inflation* – when the level of aggregate demand in the economy is rising more quickly than aggregate supply, increased competition for goods and services causes firms to raise their prices. The level of spare capacity is important in determining the degree of inflation generated from increases in aggregate demand – when there is a lot of spare capacity there is unlikely to be much inflation, as output will rise with aggregate demand.
- *Cost-push inflation* – when the price of an input in the production process increases, firms experience an increase in their costs of production. This causes them to raise prices to maintain their profits. There is likely to be significant cost-push inflation when the price of an input that accounts for a significant proportion of total costs for a significant number of firms in the economy is rising – oil prices are thus an important determinant of inflation.

Consequences of inflation

Inflation is generally considered to be harmful to an economy for the following reasons:

- *Menu costs* – when inflation is high firms have to keep amending their prices in order to reflect the higher costs of inputs. This raises a firm's costs of production.
- *Shoe leather costs* – because there tends to be a positive correlation between nominal interest rates and the rate of inflation, when there is high inflation individuals are wary of holding large cash balances (because the value of money is depreciating rapidly) and so instead choose to save more in banks to protect the real value of their money. More regular trips to the bank are therefore required because individuals want to minimise the cash balances they hold.
- *Uncertainty* – when prices are constantly changing it becomes difficult for consumers and firms to predict future circumstances, which can discourage consumption and investment. This is more likely in situations of **hyperinflation**.
- *Damages price signals* – the price mechanism acts as a signal to firms about how to allocate scarce resources. High inflation weakens the power of these signals as it makes it difficult for firms to tell whether prices are rising because of increased popularity or simply inflation.

Given these costs of inflation, it is perhaps surprising that the government targets 2% rather than no inflation. This can be explained by the concept of 'sticky' wages. There are a number of reasons why a firm at any one time may wish to reduce its workers' wages. However, workers are highly unlikely to accept a nominal wage cut.

> **Exam tip**
>
> A decrease in the rate of inflation does not mean prices are falling. Providing the rate of inflation remains positive it simply means prices are rising less quickly. This is known as disinflation.

> **Hyperinflation** A period of extremely high inflation, where prices are rising by at least 50% a month.

A moderate level of inflation solves this problem by allowing firms to increase the nominal wage by less than the rate of inflation, in doing so keeping workers motivated while achieving a reduction in real wage costs.

Deflation

Deflation occurs when the general level of prices in an economy is falling – in other words, when the rate of inflation is negative. This is something policy makers are keen to avoid because it can cause significant damage to an economy. If consumers expect deflation to continue they are likely to postpone purchases in the hope that such purchases will be cheaper in the future. This results in falling consumption, falling aggregate demand and as a result even greater falls in the price level, trapping an economy in a negative spiral it is difficult to get out of.

Trends in macroeconomic indicators

Major structural reform to the British economy in the early 1980s created a volatile economic climate, with de-industrialisation taking place at the same time as the power of trade unions was being weakened as a result of controversial legislation introduced by the Thatcher government. By the end of the decade a new era of prosperity was being enjoyed, with rising economic growth and falling unemployment. However, instability caused by Britain's exit from the Exchange Rate Mechanism resulted in the UK entering recession in 1992. Weak aggregate demand caused unemployment to rise above 10%, with high interest rates failing to bring down inflation below 8%.

The rebuilding process which followed saw the UK economy enter a period of unprecedented economic stability. From the mid-1990s until 2007 there was steady economic growth of 2–3%, unemployment fell until an equilibrium of around 5% was maintained, and price stability was achieved, with inflation fluctuating around the 2% target.

The global financial crisis in 2008 plunged the world economy into recession. The UK experienced a deeper and more prolonged recession than many other developed nations, largely because of its high exposure to the financial sector. Output fell by approximately 5% per annum in 2009 and 2010, with unemployment rising to 8%. While inflation initially fell to 1% as would be expected during a time of weak aggregate demand, rising commodity prices pushed up prices well above target, reaching a peak of 5% in 2011. The government implemented policies of fiscal austerity in an attempt to reduce the significant budget deficit. This resulted in an initially sluggish recovery, with weak GDP growth seen in the UK at a time when much faster growth was seen in Germany and the USA.

Since 2013, growth in the UK economy has been accelerating. In 2014 GDP increased by more than 3%, making Britain the fastest growing economy in the G7 (a group of seven major advanced economies). This was in stark contrast to the Eurozone economies, most of which struggled to achieve any significant positive growth. While not returning to pre-recession levels, the unemployment rate of 6% in the UK in 2014 was also substantially lower than in many competitor economies; countries such as Spain have for some years had persistent unemployment above 20%.

Exam tip

Make sure you keep up to date with what is happening in the world economy by regularly watching and reading the news – you will be expected to have current knowledge of the state of the UK economy in comparison with that of other economies for the exam.

The growth story of emerging economies since 2000 has been a key feature of the world economy in recent years. The BRIC economies of Brazil, Russia, India and China saw annual growth rates averaging in excess of 10% for a decade, which continued when the developed nations fell into recession during the global financial crisis. In recent years growth rates in these economies have slowed, averaging approximately 5%. Inflation has been rising, with supply-side capacity constraints being reached in some sectors.

There is debate among economists as to whether the BRIC nations will again return to double-digit growth rates. While some argue these economies will stabilise to achieve the more moderate growth rates of 3–4% seen in developed nations, others argue the relatively low GDP per capita means there is still potential for high growth in the future. Close attention will be paid to the performance of the MINT economies (Mexico, Indonesia, Nigeria and Turkey) over the coming years, with many economists tipping them to become the next growth story in the world economy.

Knowledge check 10

Explain how the inflation experienced by the UK economy in 2011 differed from that experienced by the BRIC nations.

Summary

After studying the topic of *Economic policy objectives and indicators of macroeconomic performance* you should be able to:

- Explain what is meant by economic growth, unemployment and inflation.
- Understand why economic growth, full employment and price stability are important macroeconomic policy objectives.
- Explain how economic growth, unemployment and inflation are measured and evaluate the difficulties associated with these measurements.
- Understand the difference between real and nominal growth.
- Explain the difference between short-run and long-run economic growth.
- Evaluate the causes of economic growth, unemployment and inflation.
- Evaluate the costs and benefits of economic growth, unemployment and inflation.
- Understand what is meant by and the impact of recessions, deflation and disinflation.
- Calculate the rate of inflation using index numbers.
- Explain the key trends in UK macroeconomic performance in the last 20 years.
- Discuss the macroeconomic performance of the UK in comparison with that of other developed economies and emerging and developing economies.

Aggregate demand and aggregate supply

Circular flow of income

The circular flow of income is a simple model which shows the flows in an economy that take place between households and firms.

As illustrated in Figure 2, households provide firms with labour. Firms pay households for this labour with income. Households then spend this income on purchasing goods and services, which are then provided to households by firms.

Exam tip

Make sure you can distinguish between physical and monetary flows in the circular flow model. In Figure 2 the monetary flows are shown by the black arrows (the income firms provide to households and the money households spend on goods and services) and the physical flows are shown by the blue arrows (the labour households supply to firms and the goods and services firms supply to households).

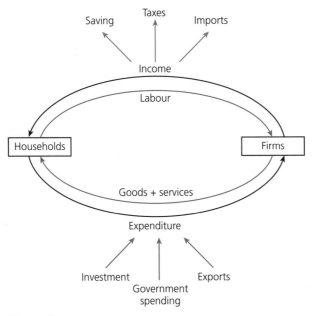

Figure 2

The circular flow model demonstrates that there are three ways of measuring national income, all of which should deliver identical results:

- *Income method* – measures the total income households receive from the different factors of production. This is comprised of wages and salaries (reward for labour), profits (reward for capital), rent (reward for land) and any income from self-employment (reward for enterprise).
- *Output method* – measures the value of the total output produced in the economy, which is comprised of output from the primary, secondary and tertiary sectors.
- *Expenditure method* – measures total expenditure in the economy, which is comprised of consumer spending, investment, government spending, exports and imports.

This generates the national income identity of:

Income = Output = Expenditure

Injections and leakages

The national income identity holds only in a closed model of the economy. In reality, expenditure from households is not the only income firms receive; they also receive income from other sources. Represented by the green arrows in Figure 2, these are known as *injections*:

- *Investment* – firms purchase goods and services in order to expand their productive capacity.
- *Government spending* – the government demands a variety of goods and services to provide to the public.
- *Exports* – spending by foreign consumers on domestic goods and services represents additional expenditure being injected into the circular flow.

Moreover, not all income generated from supplying labour flows directly to households to spend on goods and services. Represented by the red arrows in Figure 2, these outflows are known as *leakages*:

- *Saving* – consumers will choose to save rather than spend some of their income. The proportion of disposable income consumers spend is known as the average propensity to consume (APC). The average propensity to save is calculated by (1 – APC).
- *Taxes* – consumers have to give some of their income to the government in the form of taxes.
- *Imports* – consumers choose to spend some of their income on the purchase of goods and services from abroad; this represents money leaving the circular flow.

The multiplier effect

The multiplier effect proposed by Keynes suggests that initial increases in expenditure can generate greater final changes in equilibrium output. Suppose the government decides to spend £500 million building a new hospital. This injection into the circular flow directly increases output by £500 million, but it also generates additional income for the builders who build the hospital and the additional doctors who are hired to work in the hospital. These households will choose to spend some of their additional income on goods and services, generating more income for the owners of businesses these households are consuming from. These owners will choose to spend some of their additional income, causing more money to flow around the circular flow and generating an increase in total output in excess of £500 million.

The size of the multiplier effect is determined by the size of leakages. This is summarised by the **marginal propensity to withdraw**.

This is comprised of:

- *Marginal propensity to save* – the proportion of additional income that is saved, which is calculated by dividing the change in saving by the change in income. For example, if an individual's income rises by £1,000 and they choose to save £300 of this, the marginal propensity to save is equal to 0.3.
- *Marginal propensity to tax* – the proportion of additional income that is given to the government in the form of taxation, which is calculated by dividing the change in tax paid by the change in income.

Knowledge check 11

An individual who earns £30,000 a year saves £5,500. Calculate the average propensity to consume and the average propensity to save.

Knowledge check 12

What must the relationship between injections and leakages be for the macroeconomy to be in equilibrium?

Marginal propensity to withdraw The proportion of each extra pound of income which is not spent by households. This is equal to marginal propensity to save + marginal propensity to tax + marginal propensity to import.

- *Marginal propensity to import* – the proportion of additional income that is spent on the import of goods and services, which is calculated by dividing the change in expenditure on imports by the change in income. When this is high it means individuals are spending most of their additional income on imports.

The multiplier can be calculated by:

$\quad$ 1 ÷ Marginal propensity to withdraw

Therefore, the higher the marginal propensity to withdraw, the smaller the multiplier effect. In other words, when individuals face high tax rates and spend a lot of their additional income either on consuming foreign goods and services or on saving, the change in total output resulting from the initial change in total expenditure will be small, as little of the change in income that results from the initial change in expenditure will remain in the circular flow.

The concept of the multiplier is important as it helps explain the effectiveness of government expenditure in stimulating the economy. Clearly, when there is a large multiplier, the government does not need to spend a significant amount to cause a large increase in total output, making the policy effective in such circumstances.

Aggregate demand

Aggregate demand represents the total demand for goods and services produced in an economy at a given price level in any given time period. It is represented by the equation:

$\quad AD = C + I + G + (X - M)$

where C = consumption, I = investment, G = government spending, X = exports and M = imports.

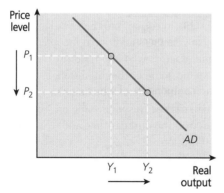

Figure 3

As shown in Figure 3, the aggregate demand curve is downward sloping. There are three theories which explain this inverse relationship between the price level and total demand in an economy:

- *Wealth effect* – a fall in the price level from P_1 to P_2 increases the amount of goods and services that individuals can afford to buy with the same income, increasing consumption and causing an extension along the aggregate demand curve, resulting in an increase in real output from Y_1 to Y_2.

Knowledge check 13

If the marginal propensity to consume is 0.8, the marginal propensity to tax is 0.3 and the marginal propensity to import is 0.1, calculate the size of the multiplier effect.

- *Interest rate effect* – when the price level falls, individuals need to borrow less to consume the same amount of goods and services. This reduces the demand for borrowing and as a result causes the interest rate to fall. When interest rates fall, consumption and investment will rise as the cost of borrowing has fallen. This causes an extension along the aggregate demand curve and an increase in real output.
- *International trade effect* – a decrease in the price level from P_1 to P_2 will improve the price competitiveness of domestic products. This will lead to an increase in demand from foreign consumers and also an increase in demand from domestic consumers, who reduce their spending on foreign goods and services as domestic products are now relatively cheaper. This improvement in net exports causes an extension along the aggregate demand curve and an increase in real output from Y_1 to Y_2.

Knowledge check 14

Explain the impact of the international trade effect when the price level increases.

Shifts in aggregate demand

An increase in aggregate demand would cause the aggregate demand curve to shift to the right. This is shown in Figure 4.

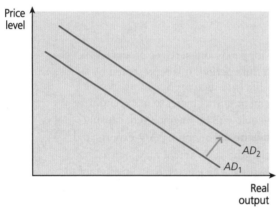

Figure 4

This can happen as a result of an increase in any of the components of aggregate demand. We consider the determinants of each of these below.

Consumption

The following factors would cause consumption to increase:

- *Increase in real disposable income* – as income rises individuals can afford to spend more on goods and services. The consumption function charts a positive relationship between real income and consumer expenditure.
- *Increase in wealth* – if the value of assets, such as houses and shares, held by individuals increases, consumption increases because confidence increases, encouraging individuals to spend some of their wealth or borrow against it.
- *Decrease in interest rates* – when interest rates fall, the opportunity cost of spending (the interest individuals could have earned from saving) falls. Borrowing also becomes cheaper and falling mortgage interest payments cause individuals to have a higher real disposable income. All of these reasons cause consumption to increase when interest rates fall.

■ *Expectations of high inflation in the future* – if individuals expect prices to rise in the future they are likely to bring forward future purchases and increase current consumption, knowing goods and services will be less expensive now than in the future.

Investment

The following factors would cause investment to increase:

■ *Decrease in interest rates* – most investment by firms is funded by borrowing. When the rate of interest falls, the cost of borrowing falls, meaning firms find investment more profitable and investment increases.

■ *Positive expectations about the future* – firms will invest to increase their productive capacity only if they believe demand for their product will rise in the future. When they anticipate rising demand they are thus more likely to invest.

■ *Reduction in corporation tax* – a decrease in corporation tax means firms get to keep a greater proportion of their profits. This increases the potential return from investment and therefore causes investment to increase.

■ *Operating close to full capacity* – when a firm is operating close to full capacity it is more likely to invest as this is the only way it will be able to increase its level of output.

Government spending

The following factors would cause government spending to increase:

■ *Economy enters recession* – the government is likely to increase spending in such instances to stimulate the economy. Some element of this increase in expenditure will be automatic – during a recession more people will be unemployed, causing the government to spend more on out-of-work benefits.

■ *Political motivation* – ahead of a general election the government may increase its level of spending to improve the standard of living of the electorate in an attempt to win votes.

Net exports

The following factors would cause net exports to increase:

■ *Decrease in the exchange rate* – this will mean foreign consumers have to swap less of their currency for each pound purchased. This makes domestic products relatively cheaper, increasing exports. Moreover, domestic consumers have to swap more pounds for each unit of a foreign currency, making imports more expensive and reducing imports.

■ *Decrease in the rate of inflation* – if the rate of inflation domestically is lower than the rate of inflation abroad, this means domestic prices are rising less quickly than foreign prices. This improves the price competitiveness of domestic products, increasing exports and reducing imports.

■ *Decrease in domestic income* – as imports are luxury goods, when incomes fall, domestic consumers can afford to buy fewer imports, reducing imports and thus increasing net exports.

■ *Increase in incomes abroad* – when foreign consumers experience an increase in income they will be able to demand more goods from abroad, increasing exports and thus increasing net exports.

Knowledge check 15

Why might consumer confidence impact on the level of consumption?

Knowledge check 16

Why might government spending actually fall during a recession?

Aggregate supply

Aggregate supply is the total output of goods and services in an economy that producers are willing and able to supply at different price levels in a given time period.

Short-run aggregate supply

In the short run, the aggregate supply curve will be upward sloping, as shown in Figure 5. This is because an increase in the price level from P_1 to P_2 makes production more profitable, which encourages firms to increase output from Y_1 to Y_2 by employing more productive factors of production or paying existing factors of production overtime pay.

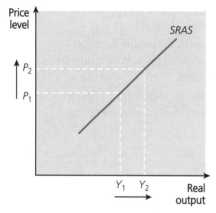

Figure 5

Shifts in short-run aggregate supply

Changes in business costs are the primary determinants of aggregate supply in the short run. This is because anything that causes production to become less profitable at any given price level will cause the aggregate supply curve to shift to the left from $SRAS_1$ to $SRAS_2$, as illustrated in Figure 6.

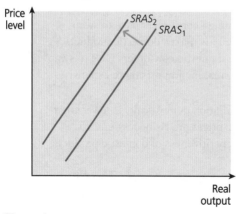

Figure 6

For example, an increase in the cost of raw materials will increase costs of production and shift the short-run aggregate supply curve to the left. The more significant the raw material is to the production of firms in the economy, the greater the shift in short-run aggregate supply will be. This explains why fluctuations in oil prices have such a significant impact on short-run aggregate supply. Moreover, increased regulation imposed on firms, such as the need to produce in a more environmentally friendly manner, can also reduce the profitability of production and therefore cause short-run aggregate supply to shift inwards.

Long-run aggregate supply

In the long run, aggregate supply in an economy is determined by the quality and quantity of its factors of production. The monetarist approach to aggregate supply argues the price level has no impact on output in the long run, as equilibrium output always converges to the productive capacity of the economy. This results in an entirely vertical long-run aggregate supply curve, as illustrated in Figure 7, with Y^* representing maximum output.

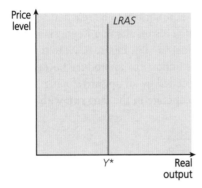

Figure 7

Shifts in long-run aggregate supply

The long-run aggregate supply curve can shift as a result of changes in the quality or quantity of factors of production. An increase in long-run aggregate supply is equivalent to an outward shift of the PPF (production possibility frontier), as it represents an increase in the economy's productive capacity. This is illustrated in Figure 8.

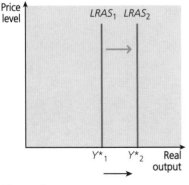
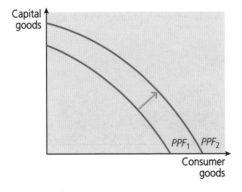

Figure 8

Examples of factors that would cause the long-run aggregate supply curve to shift to the right can be seen in the table on page 24.

the table on page 24.

Factor of production	Increase in quantity	Increase in quality
Labour	An increase in the retirement age, an increase in birth rate	Education and training could cause labour productivity to rise
Capital	Net investment – purchase of extra capital goods	Advances in technology
Land	Discovery of new oil fields	Productivity of land can be improved, e.g. through fertilisers on farmland
Enterprise	Removal of red tape, privatisation, introduction of incentives by the government	Management training and improved education

Keynesian long-run aggregate supply

The shape of the long-run aggregate supply curve is hotly debated by economists. The Keynesian school of thought argues that in reality there is a degree of inflexibility in the macroeconomy, which means it is possible for an equilibrium to be reached where the economy is not operating at maximum output. This results in a Keynesian long-run aggregate supply curve being represented as illustrated in Figure 9. Note that the vertical section of the AS curve remains at Y^* – it is impossible to produce beyond the productive capacity of the economy – but this is preceded by an upward sloping section illustrating that it is possible for the economy to operate in the long run with a degree of spare capacity.

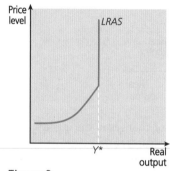

Figure 9

Macroeconomic equilibrium

Figure 10 illustrates equilibrium in the macroeconomy, where aggregate supply is equal to aggregate demand.

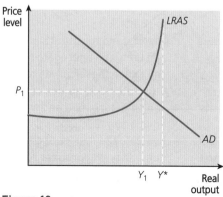

Figure 10

The equilibrium price level is at P_1, with equilibrium output at Y_1. Because output is below maximum output (Y^*) here, it is likely that there is some unemployment in the economy.

The macroeconomic equilibrium can change as a result of shifts in either the aggregate demand or the aggregate supply curve, which can occur for the reasons previously explained.

For example, suppose there is an increase in real disposable income in the economy. Because consumers can now afford to purchase more goods and services, consumption will increase, causing the aggregate demand curve to shift to the right from AD_1 to AD_2 as illustrated in Figure 11. This will generate inflation, with the price level increasing from P_1 to P_2, and will result in economic growth, with real output increasing from Y_1 to Y_2. Unemployment will fall as the derived demand for labour will increase – more workers will be needed to produce this higher level of output.

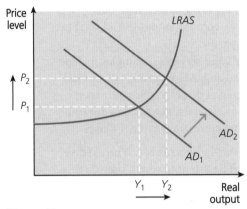

Figure 11

Knowledge check 18

Using an appropriate diagram, explain the impact of population growth on economic growth, unemployment and inflation.

Summary

After studying the topic of *Aggregate demand and aggregate supply* you should be able to:
- Understand the income, output and expenditure methods of measuring national income.
- Draw the circular flow of income, distinguishing between physical and monetary flows.
- Explain what is meant by injections and withdrawals and be able to calculate the average and marginal propensities to consume and save.
- Calculate the marginal propensity to withdraw using the marginal propensity to save, the marginal rate of tax and the marginal propensity to import.
- Explain the role and impact of the multiplier effect.
- Explain what is meant by aggregate demand and aggregate supply.

- Draw the aggregate demand and aggregate supply curves on a diagram and be able to explain their relationship with the price level.
- Explain the determinants of aggregate demand and understand how changes in these determinants cause the aggregate demand curve to shift.
- Understand the difference between short-run and long-run aggregate supply and explain what can cause these curves to shift.
- Illustrate how equilibrium in the macroeconomy can be determined and what can cause the equilibrium to change.
- Evaluate the impact of changes in aggregate demand and aggregate supply on economic growth, inflation and unemployment.

■ The application of policy instruments

Fiscal policy

Fiscal policy involves decisions made by the government on taxation and spending in order to influence the level of aggregate demand in the economy.

Taxation

There are a number of different taxes the government uses to collect revenue to finance its expenditure. These can be split into two broad categories:

- *Direct taxes* – taxes levied on income or profits, which cannot be avoided. Examples include income tax (which accounts for 32% of total tax revenue), national insurance contributions (22% of total tax revenue), corporation tax (8% of total tax revenue) and inheritance tax (0.7% of total tax revenue).
- *Indirect taxes* – taxes levied on spending on goods and services. Examples include VAT (which accounts for 21% of total tax revenue) and excise duties (11% of total tax revenue). These excise duties are often targeted at demerit goods or markets in which there are negative externalities – such as alcohol and tobacco – meaning they serve the dual purpose of raising revenue and correcting market failure.

In addition to raising revenue and dealing with market failure, taxes can be used to improve the distribution of income in an economy. The extent to which they do this depends upon the nature of the tax:

- *Progressive taxes* – take a larger percentage of the income of high earners than the income of low earners and therefore serve to reduce income inequality. Direct taxes tend to be progressive taxes. For example, individuals earning less than £12,000 a year pay no income tax, with the rate of income tax increasing as income increases, to a top rate of income tax which in 2015 stood at 45% for all income earned above £150,000.
- *Regressive taxes* – take a larger percentage of the income of low earners than the income of high earners and therefore serve to increase income inequality. Indirect taxes tend to be regressive because they charge all consumers the same tax regardless of their income. For example, goods that are subject to excise duties tend to take up a higher proportion of the income of low earners than that of high earners.

Features of a good tax system

When deciding which taxes to use to raise revenue, the government will seek to implement taxes that meet the following criteria which Adam Smith proposed as features of a good tax:

- *Equity* – taxes should be fair and be proportional to individuals' ability to pay. Corporation tax fits this principle as those firms that are generating the largest profits pay the most tax.
- *Certainty* – individuals and firms should know exactly how much tax they are expected to pay and when they are expected to pay it and the government should know exactly how much tax it expects to receive. This principle helps all economic agents to plan for the future.

Knowledge check 19

What do you think is meant by a proportional tax? Can you think of any examples?

- *Convenience* – it must be simple and easy for individuals and firms to pay their taxes. For example, VAT is easy to pay because it is simply included in the price of a good.
- *Economy* – the cost of collection must be as small as possible. There is no point implementing a tax which takes a lot from individuals but delivers little to the government because most of the tax revenue is spent on administering the tax.

Flat-rate tax system

Over the past decade a **flat-rate tax system** has been considered by a number of countries around the world, most notably Australia, whose prime minister argued it was worth exploring. Many countries, including Hungary and Estonia, already have such a system.

Proponents of such a system argue that it would significantly reduce the complexity of the current tax regime, reducing the cost of collection and making individuals more certain about the tax they are due to pay, thus meeting the certainty and economy principles. The poor would be protected as most flat-rate tax advocates propose individuals would not start paying the tax until they are earning a decent level of income, in a similar way to how the personal tax-free allowance operates in the current system. Moreover, it is argued such a system would help to improve incentives at the top end of the income distribution. Individuals on high incomes paying a marginal tax rate of 45% may not be incentivised to earn more and may even look for ways to avoid paying tax which they consider to be unfairly high. Implementing a flat tax system could therefore result in economic growth and thus increase the total tax take.

However, critics argue the flat-rate tax system goes against the most important principle at the centre of the current income tax system: equity. Income tax is used as an important tool to redistribute income in the economy; this redistribution would stop under a flat tax model. Moreover, given the top 10% of earners currently pay almost 60% of the total income tax received by the government, introducing a flat tax system would inevitably mean those on average incomes would pay more than they do at present, thus worsening their standard of living.

Government spending

The government uses its tax revenue to provide a range of public services and to support particular groups of individuals in society. The main areas of government spending are:

- healthcare – 18% of government spending
- pensions – 17% of government spending
- welfare – 16% of government spending
- education – 13% of government spending
- defence – 7% of government spending

Since the 2008 financial crisis, an interesting feature of government expenditure has been the steep increase in spending on debt interest payments. In 2014 this exceeded £50 billion – accounting for approximately 8% of total government spending.

Flat-rate tax system A system of income tax in which taxpayers pay the same rate of tax on their income.

Exam tip

It is important to understand the difference between current expenditure – spending on consumables, which has no lasting impact on the economy – and capital expenditure – spending on assets, which improves the long-run productive capacity of the economy.

Government budget

The government budget is a record of the government's income (tax revenue) and expenditure (government spending). There are three possible positions the government budget can be in:

- *budget surplus* – where tax revenue exceeds government spending
- *budget deficit* – where government spending exceeds tax revenue
- *balanced budget* – where tax revenue equals government spending

Because the government's capital expenditure is considered investment which delivers long-term benefits to the economy, the government often reports its budget position on current expenditure. As the former Chancellor Gordon Brown argued, it was acceptable for the government to operate an overall budget deficit providing there was no deficit on current expenditure – i.e. borrowing is acceptable only as a means of financing investment.

Automatic stabilisers

Without any direct action by the government, its budget adjusts according to the economic climate due to automatic stabilisers. In a recession there will be a reduction in tax revenues because fewer people are paying income tax, and because people are spending less, tax receipts from indirect taxes fall. Moreover, spending will automatically increase as more individuals will be claiming welfare benefits. This means the government is likely to run a budget deficit during a recession. The reverse is true during a boom, when tax revenues will automatically increase and welfare spending will fall.

Budget deficit and national debt

The budget deficit represents the annual amount the government has to borrow in order to finance its expenditure – it is the difference between government expenditure and tax revenue in any one year. This is known as the public sector net cash requirement (PSNCR).

National debt represents the accumulation of past borrowing. Each year the government is required to pay interest to service its debt. This debt can be reduced over time when there is a budget surplus.

The consequences of government debt

Following the 2008 global financial crisis, national debt became a concern for many of the world's advanced economies. With the UK's budget deficit exceeding £100 billion, national debt was increasing rapidly. In 2015 it exceeded £1,400 billion, which was approaching 80% of GDP.

There are a number of reasons why large national debt can be considered problematic:

- *High debt interest payments* – in 2015 the government was spending in excess of £50 billion a year on debt interest payments. There is a significant opportunity cost to such expenditure – more money spent on debt interest means less is available to spend on valuable public services.
- *Wasteful government spending* – persistent budget deficits suggest the government is living beyond its means, with some critics attributing this to wasteful spending. This could force the government to enact painful and drastic spending cuts to reduce the size of the deficit.

Knowledge check 20

What is the difference between the government's cyclical and structural budget position? Which is more damaging, a cyclical or a structural deficit?

■ *Potential tax rises* – unless the government reduces the deficit through spending cuts alone, tax increases might be required. This could harm incentives and individuals' material standard of living.

While the above points can be considered manageable, debt becomes a significant problem when it becomes unsustainable. This occurs when lenders believe there is a genuine risk that the country will be unable to finance its debt. The result is that they either become unwilling to lend or will do so only at significantly higher interest rates. This can put a country on the verge of bankruptcy, as happened to Greece in 2010, which was saved only by a bail-out by other EU nations.

However, while this level of debt is undoubtedly problematic, some economists argue the smaller level of debt seen in the UK is not a cause for serious concern. In reality, unless governments find themselves in the position of Greece, they will never be required to pay back their debt, instead seeing its real value diminish over time with inflation and economic growth. Moreover, providing the borrowing is being used to stimulate the economy and generate long-run growth, running a deficit in the short run can actually lead to debt falling in the long run by generating automatic stabilisers which result in a budget surplus in the future.

Exam tip

What level of debt classes as being 'unsustainable' is debatable. National debt of 50% of GDP is normal. UK debt close to 80% of GDP is considered undesirable but not a crisis, while Greece's debt to GDP ratio of 146% in 2010 was well beyond the point of manageable.

Expansionary fiscal policy

In order to stimulate the economy, the government might enact expansionary fiscal policy. This involves either cutting taxes or raising government spending, which will either increase the size of the budget deficit or reduce the size of the budget surplus.

For example, suppose the government reduced the basic rate of income tax. This would increase consumers' real disposable income, increasing consumption because individuals could now afford to buy more goods and services. As consumption is a component of aggregate demand, this causes the aggregate demand curve to shift to the right from AD_1 to AD_2, as illustrated in Figure 12. A multiplier effect is also likely to exist, as the income of individuals providing the additional goods and services consumed will increase, causing further increases in consumption and therefore further increases in aggregate demand to AD_3.

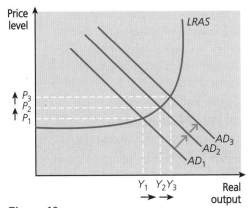

Figure 12

This policy will be effective in achieving economic growth, as real output increases from Y_1 to Y_3. Unemployment is also likely to fall, as the derived demand for labour will increase as more workers will be needed to produce the higher level of output demanded.

However, inflation is also likely to result, with prices increasing from P_1 to P_3. Moreover, the current account could be harmed, as increasing individuals' incomes will result in an increase in imports. In an economic climate where the government is concerned about rising national debt, it may be that increasing the budget deficit in this way is in any event not a viable option.

Contractionary fiscal policy

In order to reduce the size of the budget deficit or increase the size of the budget surplus, the government may choose to either increase taxes or reduce government spending. For example, it may decide to shut down a number of publicly owned leisure centres.

Because government spending is a component of aggregate demand, a decrease in government spending will cause the aggregate demand curve to shift to the left from AD_1 to AD_2, as illustrated in Figure 13. A negative multiplier effect is also likely to exist, as the income of individuals previously employed by the leisure centres will fall, causing consumption to fall and aggregate demand to fall further to AD_3.

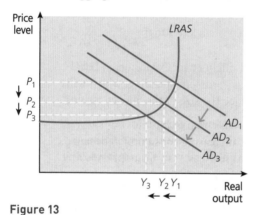

Figure 13

This will be effective in reducing inflationary pressures, with the price level falling from P_1 to P_3. Moreover, decreases in income may also improve the current account, as expenditure on imports is likely to fall. However, this will clearly harm economic growth, with real output falling from Y_1 to Y_3 and unemployment rising as the derived demand for labour will fall.

Fiscal rules

Fiscal rules represent self-imposed constraints set by the government on spending and borrowing. The 1997 Labour government formulated two such policy rules:

■ Current spending should be met out of current revenues over the course of the economic cycle – i.e. there should be no structural deficit on current expenditure.
■ Government debt should never exceed 40% of GDP.

Rules of this sort can be seen to affect the behaviour of economic agents. From the perspective of individuals and firms, such rules could encourage them to be more confident, as they believe the macroeconomy is being managed soundly. Such confidence could result in increased consumer spending and investment by firms. Moreover, these rules can help governments avoid the temptation of manipulating fiscal policy to achieve politically desirable outcomes, which could improve the sustainability of economic growth and avoid harmful fluctuations in economic performance.

However, fiscal rules clearly have any impact only if they are credible. Given the government broke both of these rules after the 2008 financial crisis, it is unlikely consumers or firms would have much faith in any new rules established in the future. Some argue that the fact the rules needed to be broken demonstrates they are not flexible enough to respond to economic circumstances and that such constraints are unhelpful in managing the economy.

Monetary policy

Monetary policy involves changing the interest rate and the money supply in order to influence the level of aggregate demand in the economy. It is primarily used to control the rate of inflation. Since 1997, the Bank of England has been responsible for the implementation of monetary policy. It operates independently of the government but is required to make decisions which result in achieving the inflation target set by the government of 2%. If inflation in any one month is beyond 1% above or below this target, the Governor of the Bank of England has to write a letter to the Chancellor explaining why the target has not been met.

The main advantage of inflation targeting is that it improves the credibility of monetary policy. When economic agents believe the central bank is committed to achieving an inflation target this is likely to reduce uncertainty, which should encourage consumption and investment and boost economic growth. Moreover, having monetary policy operating independently of the government prevents the government manipulating the interest rate to suit its political needs, again improving economic stability.

Interest rates

Adjusting interest rates represents the most commonly used tool of monetary policy. The Monetary Policy Committee meets monthly to set the bank rate of interest. If the committee members believe the economy is overheating and inflation is in danger of exceeding the target, they are likely to raise the bank rate of interest. Because commercial banks engage in numerous transactions with the central bank, an increase in the bank rate of interest is likely to feed through to the real economy as commercial banks will also raise their interest rates.

When the interest rate increases a number of things happen:

- Opportunity cost of spending (the interest which could be earned from saving) increases, meaning individuals choose to save more and spend less, causing consumption to fall.
- The cost of borrowing increases, meaning individuals borrow less and so consume less.
- Mortgage interest rates increase, decreasing real disposable income. Individuals can therefore afford to consume fewer goods and services, causing consumption to fall.
- Firms find it more expensive to borrow. Given firms borrow to fund investment, this reduces the return from investment and causes investment to fall.

Knowledge check 22

What is the difference between a symmetric and an asymmetric inflation target? Which type of target does the UK have?

Knowledge check 23

Why might the argument that a reduction in the central bank interest rate leads to a reduction in consumption as a result of mortgage interest rates increasing not hold?

- With falling demand from consumers, firms anticipate investment will be less profitable and so invest less.
- An increase in the domestic interest rate will encourage flows of hot money into the country, as foreign investors can now get a better return from saving in the UK. This causes demand for the pound to increase, which results in the exchange rate appreciating. This will reduce the price competitiveness of UK products, decreasing the demand for exports. Domestic consumers also now find it relatively cheaper to buy from abroad, causing imports to rise. The result is that net exports fall.

As consumption, investment and net exports are all components of aggregate demand and are all falling, an increase in interest rates will therefore cause the aggregate demand curve to shift to the left, as shown in Figure 14.

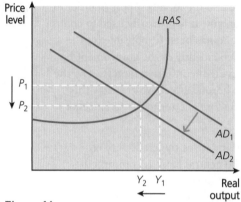

Figure 14

This causes the price level to fall from P_1 to P_2, meaning the policy is effective in reducing inflation. However, it clearly has adverse consequences on other macroeconomic objectives. As already discussed, raising interest rates is likely to worsen the balance of payments. Moreover, the fall in aggregate demand results in output falling from Y_1 to Y_2, harming economic growth. Unemployment will also increase as the demand for labour will fall. While the central bank is theoretically concerned only with controlling inflation, empirical evidence suggests it also considers the broader state of the macroeconomy when setting interest rates. This explains why interest rates were kept at an historic low of 0.5% throughout 2011 despite inflation being significantly above target, as it was felt raising interest rates would be too damaging given the fragile state of the economy.

Money supply

Since 2009, the Bank of England has been using an unconventional form of monetary policy known as **quantitative easing** in an attempt to boost consumer demand and stimulate economic growth.

While the central bank no longer has to physically print money to increase the money supply – it is all done electronically – quantitative easing has the same effect. When interest rates can go no lower this is an alternative way to stimulate spending, as purchasing these bonds from commercial banks essentially means the banks have more money. The hope is that this will increase the availability

Quantitative easing The process of purchasing assets such as government bonds to release money into the financial system.

of credit at lower interest rates, incentivising increased spending and investment. After the financial crisis the 'credit crunch' meant credit had effectively dried up – quantitative easing was designed to overcome this problem and in doing so boost aggregate demand.

However, there are limits to the effectiveness of this policy. After the financial crisis many banks were happy to keep this additional money to boost their reserves rather than use it to increase their lending. Moreover, regardless of the availability of credit, consumers and firms have to have the appetite to borrow – when confidence is low, they may not take advantage of the opportunity to undertake greater borrowing, meaning increases in aggregate demand do not materialise.

Supply-side policies

Supply-side policies consist of a range of measures designed to shift the aggregate supply curve to the right. This can be done through implementing any policy which increases either the quantity or quality of the factors of production, thereby increasing the economy's productive capacity. If successful, the policies will result in the aggregate supply curve shifting to the right from $LRAS_1$ to $LRAS_2$, as illustrated in Figure 15.

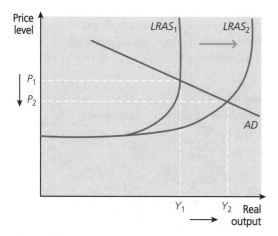

Figure 15

> **Exam tip**
>
> While not specifically supply-side policies, the demand-side policies which result in investment increasing could also shift the aggregate supply curve to the right, if they result in an increase in the quality or quantity of capital.

This will result in output increasing from Y_1 to Y_2, meaning both short-run and long-run economic growth occurs. There will also be a reduction in inflationary pressures, with the price level falling from P_1 to P_2.

While such a policy at first glance does appear very desirable, it is important to note that it will be ineffective when there is a significant amount of spare capacity in the economy. As demonstrated in Figure 16, while this will result in an improvement in the economy's productive capacity, it will have no impact on the macroeconomy in the short term, with output and prices staying the same. This perhaps explains why demand-side policies were the focus of the economic recovery following the 2008 financial crisis, as adding to what was already a significant level of spare capacity would not have helped the economy out of recession.

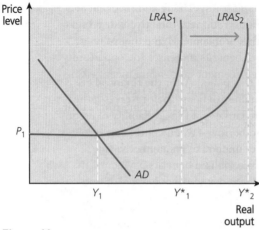

Figure 16

Education and training

Improving the human capital of workers through making them more skilled will boost the quality of labour in the economy. Recent policies aimed at effecting this include changes to the school leaving age whereby young people now have to remain in education or training until the age of 18. Record numbers of students are also now attending university. Not only does this policy involve improving individuals' academic qualifications, but funding more apprenticeships will also raise the quality of labour in an economy.

When discussing this policy it must be remembered that, as with many other supply-side policies, it is very expensive to implement. The opportunity cost of such government spending will therefore need to be closely considered.

Immigration

Immigration offers a more immediate solution to increasing the quantity of labour in an economy than an increase in the birth rate, as the economy can easily access individuals of working age. Promoting immigration is particularly beneficial when workers are highly skilled in areas in which there are skills shortages in the domestic economy – the NHS, for example, has benefited in recent years from the influx of many skilled care workers.

However, some argue the high supply of immigrants in some sectors has led to a fall in the equilibrium wage rate, displacing domestic workers and harming incentives for some individuals to participate in the labour market because they are unwilling to supply their labour at the lower equilibrium wage. This point has been made about the construction industry in recent years and is the cause of much political debate.

Improving incentives

There are a number of people in the labour market today who are voluntarily unemployed – not supplying their labour to a particular occupation because they are not incentivised to do so, believing they will be better off living on benefits. A potential policy to increase the supply of labour is to reform the tax and benefits system to incentivise more individuals to work. For example, increasing the personal allowance (the minimum income at which individuals start paying income tax) means those on low income keep a higher proportion of their income, giving them the incentive to work. Moreover, reducing out-of-work benefits increases the opportunity cost of being out of work by lowering the wage replacement ratio, again incentivising more people to work. Of course, the improved efficiency that results from such a policy has to be weighed up against potential welfare concerns that come from cutting the disposable income of society's most vulnerable citizens.

Increasing the national minimum wage is another method of widening the gap between income earned from working in a low-paid job and benefits payments. In recent years the government has encouraged firms to pay the 'living wage' to workers – this reflects the amount needed to cover the basic cost of living and varies by region – which again should incentivise labour market participation.

Reducing marginal tax rates higher up the income distribution can also increase the productive capacity of the economy by incentivising those on higher incomes to work more, as they are now able to keep a greater proportion of any additional income earned.

Flexibility

Many individuals spend a significant time out of work or in employment where they are not at their most productive because of geographical immobility. Policies to improve the mobility of labour, such as the 'Help to Buy' scheme which enables individuals to buy a house with a smaller deposit than would normally be required, will boost the flexibility of the UK labour market and in doing so may increase the productive capacity of the economy.

This can also be done through trade union reform. Trade unions have historically been seen to make it more difficult for workers to move between jobs and for firms to make adjustments to maximise their efficiency. In the 1980s legislation designed to reduce the power of trade unions therefore improved the flexibility of the economy and caused the productive capacity to increase as a consequence.

Incentivising investment

Encouraging firms to invest can improve both the quality and the quantity of capital in the economy. Firms are ultimately motivated by profit, so any policy designed to increase the profit incentive will incentivise investment. One such policy is **privatisation**, which tends to result in increased investment and efficiency because managers are now motivated by profit. The privatisation of the Royal Mail in 2014 represents a recent example of this policy.

Deregulation – reducing the operating restrictions placed on firms – also has the potential to make production more profitable and can therefore incentivise investment.

Sometimes the government chooses to incentivise investment more directly, through offering investment subsidies or research and development grants. Reducing the cost of investment in this way improves the return firms will derive from such investment, again making them more likely to invest. The danger with such a policy is that the investment is not guaranteed to increase the productive capacity of the economy – the government will therefore seek to ensure that the investment is not wasted.

Knowledge check 25

What are the drawbacks associated with increasing the national minimum wage?

Privatisation The transfer of ownership of a business from the government to a privately owned entity.

Policy conflicts

The implementation of macroeconomic policy creates a number of potential conflicts between policy objectives:

- *Unemployment and inflation* – expansionary fiscal policy designed to boost the level of aggregate demand in the economy and reduce unemployment is likely to be inflationary.
- *Growth and inflation* – any demand-side policies designed to achieve economic growth will result in inflationary pressures unless the economy is operating with significant spare capacity.
- *Inflation and the balance of payments* – to reduce inflation, the Monetary Policy Committee is likely to increase interest rates. However, this will lead to inflows of hot money, which will cause the exchange rate to appreciate and subsequently harm the balance of payments.
- *Growth and the balance of payments* – when economic growth is achieved, this is likely to raise consumers' disposable income. This will increase the demand for imports and as a consequence will damage the balance of payments.
- *Growth and income and wealth equality* – improving incentives through reforming the tax and benefits system by reducing out-of-work benefits and marginal tax rates is likely to result in economic growth being achieved. However, this will come at the cost of worsening the distribution of income.

These conflicts demonstrate that operating macroeconomic policy involves a complex series of compromises. At any one time, the policy maker will need to decide which is the most pressing objective, knowing that the resulting policy could harm another objective.

> **Knowledge check 26**
>
> Which policy is likely to generate the fewest conflicts?

Summary

After studying the topic of *The application of policy instruments* you should be able to:

- Understand what is meant by the government budget and explain the difference between a budget surplus, budget deficit and balanced budget.
- Explain the difference between a budget deficit and national debt and discuss the consequences of national debt.
- Distinguish between current and capital expenditure and know the difference between the cyclical and structural budget positions.
- Identify the different sources of tax revenue, including understanding what is meant by direct and indirect and progressive and regressive taxes, and be able to evaluate the effectiveness of a flat tax in light of the features of a 'good' tax.
- Understand the difference between automatic stabilisers and discretionary fiscal policy.
- Evaluate how discretionary fiscal policy can be used to improve macroeconomic performance.

- Explain what is meant by fiscal rules and evaluate their effectiveness.
- Explain the importance of an inflation target and understand how a central bank works to achieve this target.
- Understand the different monetary policy techniques, including interest rate adjustments and quantitative easing.
- Evaluate how monetary policy can be used to improve macroeconomic performance.
- Explain a range of supply-side policies designed to increase the productive capacity of the economy, including education and training, improving incentives and flexibility, encouraging investment and promoting immigration.
- Evaluate how supply-side policies can be used to improve macroeconomic performance.
- Explain a range of possible trade-offs that result from macroeconomic policy and evaluate the consequences for policy makers of these trade-offs.

The global context

International trade

International trade involves the exchange of goods and services between countries. It is comprised of:

- *Exports* – domestically produced goods and services purchased by foreign consumers in exchange for money flowing from the foreign country to the domestic economy.
- *Imports* – goods and services produced abroad and consumed domestically in exchange for money flowing from the domestic economy to the foreign country.

Absolute advantage

A country is said to have an absolute advantage over another country in the production of a good or service when it can produce it using fewer resources than another country.

Imagine there are two countries, A and B, producing televisions and cars. If they each decided to concentrate all of their resources on the production of one of these products, they could produce the following quantities:

- specialising in televisions – Country A: 5,000 TVs, Country B: 1,000 TVs
- specialising in cars – Country A: 500 cars, Country B: 2,500 cars

It is clear to see here that Country A has an absolute advantage in the production of televisions and Country B has an absolute advantage in the production of cars.

Before specialisation, assume the countries decide to divide their resources equally between the production of televisions and cars:

- Country A: 2,500 TVs, 250 cars
- Country B: 500 TVs, 1,250 cars

This would deliver a total output of 3,000 TVs and 1,500 cars. If the countries each specialise in producing the good they have an absolute advantage in, production will be as follows:

- Country A: 5,000 TVs
- Country B: 2,500 cars

Assuming the countries share this output equally between them, they will be able to enjoy the following consumption levels:

- Country A: 2,500 TVs, 1,250 cars
- Country B: 2,500 TVs, 1,250 cars

This demonstrates that both countries will gain from trade.

Comparative advantage

Now imagine two other countries, C and D, producing eggs and t-shirts.

If they each decided to concentrate all of their resources on the production of one of these products, they could produce the following quantities:

- specialising in eggs – Country C: 10,000 eggs, Country D: 5,000 eggs
- specialising in t-shirts – Country C: 5,000 t-shirts, Country D: 1,000 t-shirts

Knowledge check 27

Why would it be unwise for any country to specialise in the production of one product?

In this case, Country C has an absolute advantage in the production of both eggs and t-shirts. However, the theory of **comparative advantage** demonstrates how these countries can still benefit from trade.

Opportunity cost ratios

The theory of comparative advantage can be understood by considering the opportunity cost faced by each country in the production of these goods. The opportunity cost of Country C producing an egg is the sacrifice of 0.5 t-shirts. The opportunity cost of Country D producing an egg is the sacrifice of 0.2 t-shirts.

Therefore, Country D is relatively more efficient at producing eggs than t-shirts – the opportunity cost of it producing eggs is lower than it is for Country C. If Country D therefore specialises in the production of eggs and Country C specialises in the production of t-shirts, it is possible for both countries to gain from trade.

To prove these gains from trade, suppose before this specialisation takes place that the countries decide to divide their resources equally between the production of eggs and t-shirts:

- Country C: 5,000 eggs, 2,500 t-shirts
- Country D: 2,500 eggs, 500 t-shirts

This would deliver a total output of 7,500 eggs and 3,000 t-shirts. Suppose Country C, as the country with the comparative advantage in the production of t-shirts, decides to focus 70% of its resources on producing t-shirts and the other 30% of its resources on producing eggs. Country D, which does not have the absolute advantage in the production of either product but has a comparative advantage in the production of eggs, decides to focus 100% of its resources on the production of eggs.

Total output will be as follows:

- Eggs = 3,333 (Country C) + 5,000 (Country D) = **8,333**
- T-shirts = **3,500** (Country C)

The total output of both goods has increased, meaning gains from trade can be enjoyed as a result of comparative advantage.

Terms of trade

In our previous example, which country gains the most from trade depends on the relative prices at which eggs and t-shirts are exchanged. This is known as the terms of trade. Clearly, if the terms of trade in this example were two eggs for one t-shirt, then both Countries C and D would gain from trade (if C gives D 1,000 t-shirts in exchange for 2,000 eggs, C will end up with 5,333 eggs and 2,500 t-shirts and D will end up with 3,000 eggs and 1,000 t-shirts, meaning both have more output than they did before trade).

However, if the terms of trade changed and more eggs needed to be swapped for t-shirts, it could result in Country D enjoying few benefits from trade, with most of the benefits going to Country C.

The terms of trade can be affected by the market power any one country has – a country with power will be able to manipulate the terms of trade to better suit it. The fact that the terms of trade tend to change over time sends an important warning to

Knowledge check 28

Calculate the opportunity cost ratios for both countries in the production of t-shirts.

Knowledge check 29

Calculate the terms of trade in this example if Country C ends up with 6,333 eggs and 2,500 t-shirts and Country D ends up with 2,000 eggs and 1,000 t-shirts.

countries considering specialising entirely in the production of one product – while this may seem like a good idea at the time, if the terms of trade change in the future the country could lose out.

Patterns of trade

Natural resource endowments are an important explanation of patterns of trade seen across the world today. For example, the UK imports bananas because it doesn't have the climate to produce them domestically, while the Middle East region exports vast quantities of oil because of its large supply.

Continued integration in the European Union has meant trade between member countries tends to account for a significant proportion of the exports and imports of EU member states. This to an extent goes against the theory of comparative advantage, with trade taking place between nations not because of relative opportunity costs but because there are no trade barriers imposed on such trade.

The rapid growth of the Asian 'Tiger' economies has meant Asia is playing an increasingly important role in world trade. As incomes in these countries have started to rise, they are becoming more important export destinations for the developed Western economies. Meanwhile, China's export-led growth means it exports in vast quantities. Africa, however, remains on the periphery of global trade, despite its large population.

The UK is heavily reliant on the EU and the USA as trading partners – 75% of its exports goes to these countries. Its major exports consist of financial services and insurance, with the export of manufactured goods slowly declining over time, except in advanced industries such as pharmaceuticals.

Policies to achieve international competitiveness

There are a number of policies available to the government to improve international competitiveness:

- *Productivity growth* – improving education and training and/or incentivising investment can improve the rate at which firms produce output. This lowers the cost of production and makes domestic products more internationally price competitive.
- *Reducing unit labour costs* – one of the reasons China enjoys high levels of exports is its extremely low unit labour costs. In the UK it is unlikely the government would implement any policy designed to reduce wages, but productivity improvements would have the same effect of reducing unit labour costs.
- *Exchange rate depreciation* – this will mean foreign consumers have to swap less of their currency for the domestic currency, thus increasing the price competitiveness of domestic goods and services.
- *Improving product quality* – this makes the domestically produced products more desirable, increasing demand.

Exam tip

Product quality is essential for many developed nations if they are to maintain international competitiveness – realistically they will always struggle to compete on price with low-cost developing nations.

Balance of payments

The balance of payments is a set of accounts which monitors the transactions that take place between UK residents and the rest of the world. All transactions entered into the balance of payments can be categorised as a credit item (money flows into the country as a result of the transaction) or a debit item (money flows out of the country as a result of the transaction).

When everything is added together the balance of payments must 'balance' (i.e. equal zero), as ultimately all spending must be funded from somewhere. The balance of payments can be split into three components:

■ *Current account*
  – *Transactions in goods and services* – this records a country's exports and imports. The UK has a large deficit in the trade of goods which is partially offset by a surplus in the trade of services.
  – *Net investment income* – profits earned abroad by UK firms count as a credit item on this component. Any profits made by foreign firms in the UK which are repatriated represent a debit item. The UK has a surplus on this component of the current account.
  – *International transfers* – these are transfers made or received by governments or private individuals. The UK has a deficit on this component – the UK has a relatively large foreign aid budget and many immigrant workers in the UK send transfers back to family in their home countries.
■ *Capital account* – this records all capital transfers. This account is relatively small and is largely concerned with the transfer of assets of migrants. For example, when someone migrates to the UK, their property becomes part of the UK's assets. The UK runs a surplus on this component.
■ *Financial account* – this measures the transactions in financial assets, including investment flows and central government transactions in foreign exchange reserves. The UK runs a large surplus on this account, which is needed to fund the deficit on the current account – the UK sells assets to foreign investors and borrows from abroad.

Imbalances on the balance of payments

The UK has a significant deficit on the current account of the balance of payments and has done for some time. There are a number of explanations for this:

■ *Loss of comparative advantage in manufacturing* – the UK has struggled to compete with developing low labour cost countries or developed countries with more sophisticated capital. This has led to deindustrialisation and a significant deficit on the trade in goods (also known as visible trade), which is only partially offset by the surplus on the trade in services.
■ *High levels of domestic consumption* – over time incomes in the UK have been rising and there has been a growing appetite to borrow to fund more consumption. This has increased the demand for imports.
■ *A relatively high exchange rate* – this has worsened the price competitiveness of domestically produced goods and services and encouraged domestic consumers to increase their expenditure on imports.

Of course, a current account deficit does mean consumers are enjoying high levels of consumption, meaning it cannot automatically be seen as a bad thing – many of the world's countries with the highest standard of living have current account deficits. However, it becomes a problem when such deficits become unsustainable, which happens when other countries are no longer prepared to lend to the country to finance its deficit. Moreover, even if a country doesn't reach this point, a rising deficit can demonstrate underlying weakness in the competitiveness of domestic goods and services and is likely to result in unemployment.

Exam tip

A current account deficit means the value of imports exceeds the value of exports. The word 'value' is very important here – if a country was exporting 5,000 pencils but importing 1,000 televisions, then the number of exports would exceed the number of imports but there would still be a current account deficit, as televisions are much more valuable than pencils.

Knowledge check 30

If a country has a deficit in the trade of goods and services of £35.4 billion, a surplus of net investment income of £21.4 billion and a deficit of international transfers of £11.8 billion, calculate the current account balance.

Correcting imbalances on the balance of payments

There are a number of policy options available to the government to correct a current account deficit:

■ *Exchange rate depreciation* – purchasing foreign currency reserves will increase the supply of pounds, reducing the exchange rate and improving the price competitiveness of domestic goods and services.

■ *Deflationary demand management* – increasing taxes decreases disposable income and is likely to reduce expenditure on imports. The price level is also likely to fall which will improve the price competitiveness of exports.

■ *Import restrictions* – imposing protectionist policies such as tariffs and quotas could reduce the volume of imports and improve the balance of payments. If other countries retaliate, however, this could also lead to a reduction in exports.

Given the significant drawbacks that exist with all of the above policies, supply-side developments are the favoured method of improving the balance of payments. Improving the level of productivity in the economy through increasing the skill level of workers and incentivising firms to invest in research and development could achieve the dual aims of increasing the price competitiveness and improving the quality of domestic products, both of which could increase exports and reduce imports. While desirable, such policies are not straightforward to implement effectively – despite much focus on this area in recent years there have been no real improvements in the UK's current account position.

Knowledge check 31
Why is deflationary demand management unlikely to be adopted by the government to correct a balance of payments deficit?

Exchange rates

An exchange rate measures the price of one currency in terms of another currency. It is crucial in determining a country's international competitiveness and has a strong influence on a country's balance of payments position. When the exchange rate is high, it means foreign consumers have to swap a lot of their currency for domestic currency. This worsens the price competitiveness of exports. Moreover, a high exchange rate makes it relatively cheaper for domestic consumers to purchase from abroad, as a small amount of domestic currency can be exchanged for a lot of foreign currency. This means imports will be high.

Floating exchange rate system

In a floating exchange rate system, the equilibrium exchange rate is determined by the market forces of supply and demand.

■ Demand for pounds is determined by the demand for UK goods and services from foreign consumers – sterling is needed to purchase exports, so the greater the demand for exports, the greater the demand for pounds. Sterling is also demanded by foreign investors looking to save in British financial institutions.

■ Supply of pounds is determined by the demand for foreign goods and services by UK consumers. To purchase imports domestic consumers need to exchange their pounds for foreign currency, meaning there is a high supply of pounds when the demand for imports is high. The supply of pounds will also be high when domestic investors are looking to save in financial institutions abroad, causing them to want to swap pounds for foreign currency.

This generates an equilibrium exchange rate at e_1, as illustrated in Figure 17.

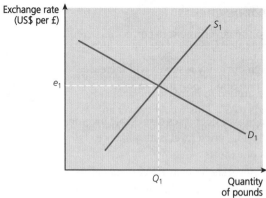

Figure 17

Any changes in the demand or supply of a currency can cause the exchange rate to change. For example, suppose there is an increase in the domestic interest rate. This causes hot money to flow into the economy, as foreign investors get a better return from saving in domestic financial institutions. This increases the demand for pounds from D_1 to D_2, as illustrated in Figure 18. This causes the exchange rate to appreciate from e_1 to e_2.

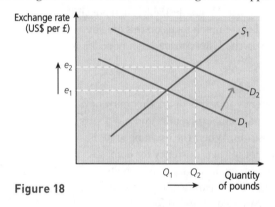

Figure 18

Knowledge check 32

Analyse the impact of an increase in foreign interest rates on the exchange rate.

Evaluating floating exchange rate systems

There are a number of arguments both for and against floating exchange rate systems:

Advantages	Disadvantages
Monetary policy can be used to stabilise the economy rather than being dictated by having to keep an exchange rate at a fixed level	Can result in macroeconomic policy indiscipline – for example, a government can pursue short-term growth causing high inflation, knowing it does not have to achieve a particular exchange rate target
Economy can easily adjust to shocks – if there is a balance of payments deficit, this means the demand for pounds will be low, which will depreciate the exchange rate and increase the demand for exports	Causes uncertainty, as firms cannot predict the exchange rate in the future. This may make them wary of signing contracts, which can reduce investment

Fixed exchange rate system

After the Second World War, at the Bretton Woods conference, a number of countries agreed to establish a **fixed exchange rate system**. Governments agreed to maintain a fixed price of their currency against the dollar, with changes in the exchange rate possible only after an agreement was reached with other countries participating in the system.

Fixed exchange rate system The government or central bank fixes the value of the currency against another currency.

Figure 19 illustrates how a fixed exchange rate system operates in practice. Suppose demand for pounds is at D_1, perhaps because there is a lack of foreign demand for UK goods and services. This will put pressure on the pound to depreciate to e_1. However, in a fixed exchange rate system, this is not possible, as the exchange rate must be maintained at e_f. To do this the government will need to sell foreign exchange reserves, in doing so buying up pounds. This can either be argued to increase the demand for pounds to D^* or decrease the supply of pounds to S^*. This would deliver an equilibrium at point B or C, meaning the fixed exchange rate would be maintained.

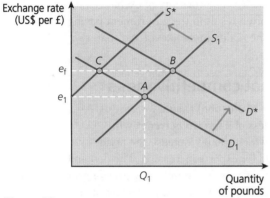

Figure 19

Knowledge check 33

Explain how a fixed exchange rate could be maintained in a situation when there was excess demand for pounds.

While such adjustments are possible in the short term, problems arise in the long term if the exchange rate is consistently under- or overvalued. This ultimately resulted in the UK leaving the Exchange Rate Mechanism (ERM) in 1992 – the pound had been overvalued for too long and the government had run out of the foreign currency reserves required to sustain its value at such a high level.

It is clear to see that in a fixed exchange rate system there is a temptation to devalue the currency to improve international price competitiveness. This has in fact been a key feature of China's growth. To sustain this, however, requires domestic production to be able to expand rapidly in line with increased demand to avoid inflation.

Evaluating fixed exchange rate systems

There are a number of arguments both for and against fixed exchange rate systems:

Advantages	Disadvantages
Reduced exchange rate uncertainty means the prices of exports and imports will be more stable, which reduces the risk of trade and investment. More confidence in future prices will make firms happier about signing long-term contracts, knowing they will not lose out as a result of exchange rate fluctuations	High levels of foreign exchange reserves are required to maintain fixed exchange rate
Imposes discipline on domestic firms, which know the only way to increase competitiveness is through productivity improvements, as the exchange rate cannot depreciate to artificially make them more competitive	Monetary policy has to be focused on maintaining exchange rate peg. For example, this could require the central bank to raise interest rates to stop depreciation pressures, which would be undesirable at a time when the government wanted to expand the economy

Hybrid exchange rate system

To enjoy the advantages of both fixed and floating exchange rate systems, some countries have tried adopting hybrid exchange rate systems. These operate by allowing the currency to float but with the government intervening occasionally as required. China has operated such a system, intervening to ensure the value of its currency remains artificially low.

The UK experimented with a hybrid exchange rate system when it joined the ERM in 1990. Here the currency was allowed to float but only within a 2.25% range of the weighted average of all member countries' currencies. The volatility of exchange rates does mean, however, that such hybrid systems often result in the government having to intervene more often than planned, making the reality more like a fixed than a floating exchange rate system.

Exchange rates and international competitiveness

Theoretically, reducing the value of a currency (devaluation) should improve international competitiveness. This is because less of a foreign currency will be needed to purchase the domestic currency, which should increase the price competitiveness of exports and result in demand for exports increasing. The demand for imports should also fall, as domestic consumers now find purchasing foreign goods and services relatively more expensive. This should improve the current account of the balance of payments. Moreover, as net exports is a component of aggregate demand, the aggregate demand curve should shift to the right from AD_1 to AD_2, as shown in Figure 20.

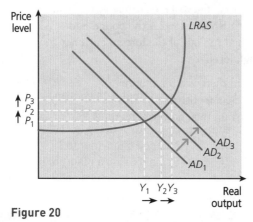

Figure 20

There is also likely to be an increase in consumption, as domestic consumers switch to buying more domestic products as they are now relatively cheaper. This causes a further increase in aggregate demand to AD_3. The result is that economic growth will take place as real output increases from Y_1 to Y_3 and there is likely to be a reduction in unemployment, as the derived demand for labour increases.

However, the J-curve effect illustrates how this analysis may not hold. This is because, in the short run, the elasticity of demand for imports and exports may be inelastic. Foreign consumers will not immediately start consuming more exports when the price competitiveness improves (it may be that this isn't possible anyway because

Knowledge check 34

Would an appreciation/ revaluation of a currency ever be desirable?

supply of exports may be inelastic in the short run) and domestic consumers will not immediately change their behaviour and decrease their consumption of imports. The result is that:

- the volume of imports will remain constant, meaning the overall value of imports rises (as imports are now relatively more expensive)
- the volume of exports will remain constant, meaning the overall value of exports falls (as exports are now relatively cheaper).

The result is that the current account deficit will worsen in the short run. This is illustrated in Figure 21. When the devaluation takes place at time period A, there is initially a worsening of the current account. It is only at point B, when the demand and supply of imports and exports have become more elastic, that an improvement in the current account is seen.

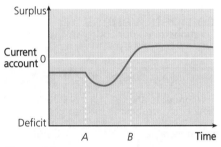

Figure 21

This analysis is summarised by the **Marshall–Lerner condition**, which details how it is only when the quantity effect fully offsets the price effect of a devaluation that there will be an improvement in the current account.

Marshall–Lerner condition For a currency devaluation to lead to an improvement in the current account, the sum of the price elasticities of demand for exports and imports must be negative and numerically greater than 1.

Summary

After studying the topic of *The global context* you should be able to:

- Distinguish between absolute and comparative advantage and calculate opportunity cost ratios to demonstrate the gains from trade.
- Calculate the terms of trade and explain how trade theories explain global patterns of trade.
- Explain how countries achieve international competitiveness.
- Identify the different components of the balance of payments and be able to calculate their balances.
- Evaluate the causes and consequences of imbalances on the balance of payments.
- Evaluate policies to correct imbalances on the balance of payments.
- Explain using a diagram how exchange rates are determined in fixed and floating exchange rate systems.
- Evaluate the relative merits and drawbacks of different exchange rate systems.
- Evaluate the impact of exchange rate changes on international competitiveness, including consideration of the J-curve effect and the Marshall–Lerner condition.

Questions & Answers

This section provides an explanation of the structure of both the AS and A-level Macroeconomics papers and strategies for approaching the different types of questions you will encounter in the exam. This is followed by a series of sample questions covering all the question types – multiple choice, data response and essays. After all of these questions there are some example answers from students. You should practise all of these questions yourself and compare your answers to these while reading the detailed exam advice to improve your understanding of what is required to achieve full marks.

Assessment objectives

To succeed in this course you will need to be able to demonstrate your ability in the following assessment objectives:

AO	Key skill	Explanation	Weighting at AS	Weighting at A-level
1	Knowledge	Demonstrate knowledge of terms/concepts and theories/models.	30%	22.5%
2	Application	Apply knowledge and understanding to various economic contexts.	30%	25%
3	Analysis	Analyse issues within economics, showing an understanding of their impact on economic agents.	20%	25%
4	Evaluation	Evaluate economic arguments and use qualitative and quantitative evidence to support informed judgements relating to economic issues.	20%	27.5%

AS macroeconomics

This is examined by a 90-minute paper. There are 60 marks awarded for the paper; you therefore have approximately 90 seconds to answer each question.

The paper is split into three sections:

- **Section A – Multiple choice**
  You will be asked 15 multiple-choice questions covering the AS Macroeconomics specification. These could require you to conduct simple calculations, interpret points on diagrams or recall knowledge about technical theory.
  Each question is worth 1 mark and you will have to select the correct answer from a choice of four options.
  You should aim to spend approximately 20 minutes on this section.
- **Section B – Data response**
  You will be given an extract focusing on the macroeconomic performance of a particular country or group of countries. You will then be asked a series of questions related to this extract which tests the full range of assessment objectives. Questions will range in value from straightforward 1 mark questions to a 10-mark question, which is level marked in the same way as the essays.

The section is worth a total of 25 marks and you should aim to spend approximately 40 minutes on it.

■ **Section C – Quantitative essay questions**

You will be given a choice of two essay questions and must answer one of these. The answer will require you to demonstrate some quantitative skills, most likely through drawing a diagram.

The essay is worth 20 marks and you should aim to spend approximately 30 minutes on it.

A-level macroeconomics

This is examined by a 120-minute paper. There are 80 marks awarded for the paper; you therefore have approximately 90 seconds to answer each question.

The content covered in the paper will include everything in this book alongside the Year 2 Macroeconomics content.

The paper is split into three sections:

■ **Section A – Data response**

You will be given a variety of stimulus material, which is most likely to focus on the macroeconomic performance of a particular country or group of countries. You will then be asked a series of questions related to this stimulus material which tests the full range of assessment objectives. Questions will range in value from straightforward 2-mark questions to an 8- and a 12-mark question, both of which are level marked in the same way as the essays.

The section is worth a total of 30 marks and you should aim to spend approximately 40 minutes on it.

■ **Section B – Quantitative essay questions**

You will be given a choice of two essay questions and must answer one of these. The answer will require you to demonstrate some quantitative skills, most likely through drawing a diagram.

The essay is worth 25 marks and you should aim to spend approximately 40 minutes on it.

■ **Section C – Qualitative essay questions**

You will be given a choice of two essay questions and must answer one of these. These essays will not require you to demonstrate any quantitative skills but you may well find a diagram will support your discussion; relevant diagrams will be credited.

The essay is worth 25 marks and you should aim to spend approximately 40 minutes on it.

Answering multiple-choice questions

When answering multiple-choice questions you should:
■ Work through them quickly – remember you have only 90 seconds on average to complete each one. Some will take longer than this but that should be compensated by others which are much quicker to complete. Do not spend too long on any one question.

- Cover up the options when reading the question and see whether you can work out the answer before looking at the four options – this is often quicker than reading the options and getting distracted by those that are incorrect but are close to being right.
- If unsure, eliminate those answers you know to be incorrect and choose between any options you have left – there is no penalty for answering incorrectly so you should never leave an answer blank.
- When practising multiple-choice questions in the build-up to the exam try to justify why the incorrect options are incorrect. This is done in the example multiple-choice questions in this guide.

Answering data-response questions

When answering data-response questions you should:

- Read the stimulus material very carefully, remembering to refer to it in your answers when required.
- Work out which assessment objectives the question is testing – do not waste time evaluating when the question is only asking you to offer an explanation.
- Make sure you always fully apply your answer to the circumstances in the question. You will need to reference the stimulus material throughout and should avoid producing bland technical answers which ignore the specific information given about the country/countries in the case study.

Answering essay questions

The most important thing to remember when answering essay questions is to cover each of the four skills tested by the assessment objectives. These essays, along with any questions which require evaluation in the data-response section, are level marked. Which level your answer is placed in depends upon how well you have covered each of the four skills – these are graded as being either 'Limited', 'Reasonable', 'Good' or 'Strong', as detailed below.

	AO1 & AO2	AO3	AO4
Limited	Awareness of the meaning of the terms in the question.	Simple statement(s) of cause and effect.	An unsupported assertion.
Reasonable	As above + applied to the context of the question	An explanation of causes and consequences, which omit some key links in the chain of argument.	Some attempt to come to a conclusion, which shows some recognition of influencing factors.
Good	Precision in the use of the terms in the question and applied in a focused way to the context of the question.	An explanation of causes and consequences, developing most of the links in the chain of argument.	A conclusion is drawn weighing up both sides, but without reaching a supported judgement.
Strong		An explanation of causes and consequences, fully developing the links in the chain of argument.	A conclusion is drawn weighing up both sides, and reaches a supported judgement.

Generally, the best way to approach these questions is to fully analyse one side of the argument, fully analyse the other side and then reach a judgement saying which side of the argument is stronger and why you have reached this conclusion. This is likely to include a consideration of the factors your judgement depends upon.

■ AS macroeconomics Section A

Multiple-choice questions

Question 1

Real GDP in an economy is equal to:

A   Total output measured at current prices

B   Total output measured at constant prices

C   Total output ÷ population

D   Population ÷ total output

Question 2

A recession is defined as:

A   A negative economic growth rate for two consecutive quarters

B   A fall in the rate of economic growth for two consecutive quarters

C   A decrease in total output in the economy for four consecutive quarters

D   A period in which the size of the population is rising faster than total output

Question 3

The working age population of a country is 55 million. The unemployment rate is 5%, with 1.2 million people unemployed. What percentage of the population is economically active?

A   95%   B   97.82%   C   43.64%   D   41.45%

Question 4

The UK government sets the Bank of England a 2% inflation target. Which measure of inflation is this target based on?

A   RPI   B   RPIX   C   CPI   D   CPIH

Question 5

Saving, taxes and imports are all examples of:

A   Leakages from the circular flow of income

B   Components of aggregate demand

C   Contractionary fiscal policy

D   Policies to achieve economic growth

Question 6

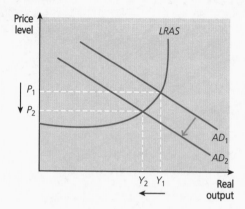

The figure above could be illustrating changes in the macroeconomic equilibrium as a result of:

A   Investment subsidies to promote research and development

B   An decrease in the personal tax allowance

C   A decrease of the interest rate

D   A depreciation of the exchange rate

Question 7

Which of the following is not a feature of a good tax?

A   Equity

B   Certainty

C   Convenience

D   Complexity

Question 8

Expansionary monetary policy be will ineffective when:

A   Nominal interest rates are close to zero

B   Commercial banks adjust their interest rates in response to changes in the base rate

C   Many households are on variable rate mortgages

D   There is a high level of confidence in the economy

Question 9

Which of the figures below illustrates the likely impact on the economy of an increase in the compulsory school leaving age?

A
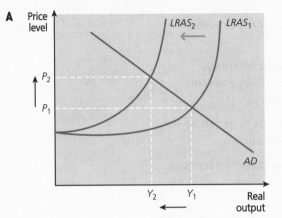

B
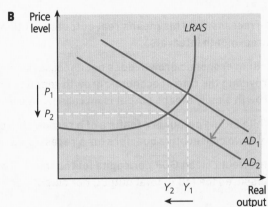

C
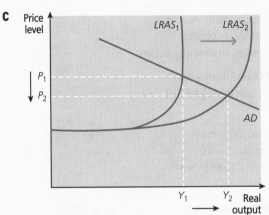

D
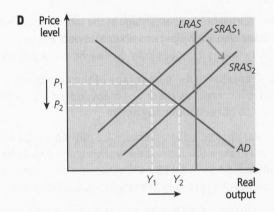

Question 10

The J-curve demonstrates that a currency depreciation:

A Worsens the current account in the short and the long run

B Improves the current account in the short and long run

C Worsens the current account in the short run and improves it in the long run

D Improves the current account in the short run and worsens it in the long run

Answers and rationale

Question 1

A This is nominal GDP – i.e. output not adjusted for inflation.

B *Correct answer.* Measuring output at constant prices strips out the effects of inflation and therefore effectively measures real output.

C This is a measure of output per head of the population – GDP per capita.

D This is not a measure used or recorded by economists.

Question 2

A *Correct answer.* This means real output has fallen in both of the previous three-month intervals.

B Falling economic growth does not necessarily mean output is falling – providing the rate of economic growth remains positive, falling economic growth simply means output is increasing at a slower rate.

C While falling output is a feature of a recession, output needs to be falling for only two consecutive quarters for a recession to be triggered.

D This would mean GDP per capita (output per head) is falling, but a recession measures the fall in total output, not output per head.

Question 3

A This represents the percentage of the labour force that is in employment – i.e. 95% of those who are willing and able to work are in work. This is not the economic activity rate as it implies individuals who are unemployed are not economically active.

B This represents the percentage of the population that is not unemployed. This is incorrect as there are many individuals who are not unemployed but are also not economically active.

C *Correct answer.* Labour force = 1.2 million ÷ 0.05 = 24 million. Economic activity rate = labour force ÷ working age population = 24 million ÷ 55 million = 43.64%. So 43.64% of the working age population is either in work (employed) or actively seeking work (unemployed).

D This answer uses the same calculation as above but takes the number of people unemployed away from the size of the labour force and uses this number to calculate the economic activity rate – i.e. it makes the assumption that individuals who are unemployed are not economically active, which is incorrect.

Question 4

A The Retail Prices Index was used until 2003 as the index upon which to base the inflation target. The main difference between this and the CPI is that it includes housing costs such as mortgage interest payments.

B This is the Retail Prices Index excluding mortgage interest payments. It is similar to the CPI but adopts a slightly different methodology, such as excluding households from the top and bottom of the income distribution.

C *Correct answer.* This is the official measure of inflation used in the UK.

D This adapts the CPI to include housing costs and is similar to the RPI.

Question 5

A *Correct answer.*

B Aggregate demand = $C + I + G + X - M$. Only imports are a component of aggregate demand. Saving and taxes have an impact on consumption, government spending and investment but are not components.

C Contractionary fiscal policy could involve increasing taxes but does not involve the direct manipulation of saving or imports.

D Reductions in saving, taxes and imports could all achieve economic growth but are not policies in themselves.

Question 6

A This would shift the aggregate supply curve to the right, increasing the productive capacity of the economy.

B *Correct answer.* This would decrease individuals' real disposable income as the income at which they start paying income tax will have fallen. This will reduce consumption and cause the aggregate demand curve to shift to the left.

C This will reduce the opportunity cost of spending and make it cheaper to borrow, increasing consumption and investment and causing the aggregate demand curve to shift to the right.

D This will increase the price competitiveness of exports, causing net exports to increase and the aggregate demand curve to shift to the right.

Question 7

A This is a feature of a good tax because it means people are charged based on their ability to pay.

B This is a feature of a good tax because it improves confidence – consumers and firms know how much tax they will have to pay and the government can predict with confidence how much tax it expects to receive.

C This is a feature of a good tax because when taxes are simple to pay they are cheaper to administer and it is less likely that people will avoid paying or pay the incorrect amount.

D *Correct answer.* A complex tax is ineffective because it causes confusion and tends to be more costly to administer, meaning the government spends too much of the revenue the tax generates administering its collection.

Question 8

A *Correct answer.* When nominal interest rates are close to zero the economy is in a liquidity trap – interest rates cannot be reduced by a meaningful enough amount to influence spending decisions. In such circumstances spending is low because of factors other than the interest rate as borrowing is already very cheap.

B This improves the effectiveness of expansionary monetary policy, as when the central bank rate changes this will be passed onto consumers and firms in the form of lower borrowing costs charged by commercial banks.

C When the interest rate falls households on variable rate mortgages will experience an immediate increase in their real disposable income, increasing consumption and therefore making expansionary monetary policy effective.

D The purpose of expansionary monetary policy is to increase consumption and investment. This is more likely to happen when individuals and firms are confident – when they are feeling hopeful about future prospects it is more likely they will respond to a change in the interest rate.

Question 9

A This diagram shows the economy's productive capacity decreasing – raising the school leaving age will increase the quality of labour so will increase the productive capacity.

B Raising the school leaving age is likely to increase government spending on education, meaning if aggregate demand is affected at all, it is likely to increase and shift to the right, as government spending is a component of aggregate demand.

C *Correct answer.* Raising the school leaving age will mean people are more skilled, thus increasing the quality of labour and therefore increasing the productive capacity of the economy, causing the long-run aggregate supply curve to shift to the right.

D This figure illustrates an increase in the short-run aggregate supply. There are a number of temporary factors that may have caused this, such as a fall in raw materials costs, but this does not illustrate any change in the productive capacity of the economy, which is what improving education does.

Question 10

A Given a depreciation improves the price competitiveness of exports, it is unlikely a currency depreciation would be expected to worsen the current account in the short and the long run.

B This would imply the volume of exports and imports changes immediately when the price changes, which is unlikely.

C *Correct answer.* In the short run the price elasticity of demand for imports and exports is likely to be inelastic. This means that when the price of exports falls as a result of a depreciation, the volume of exports doesn't increase by much in the short run, meaning the value of exports falls. Equally, when the price of imports rises, the volume of imports doesn't decrease by much, meaning the value of imports rises. This worsens the current account in the short run. In the long run, when consumers have a chance to alter their spending habits demand will become more price elastic and the current account is likely to improve as a result of the greater price competitiveness of exports.

D This is incorrect – were price elasticity of demand for exports and imports to be elastic in the short run (and so cause a short-run current account improvement), this would generate a long-run improvement as well.

■AS macroeconomics Section B

Data response

Economic crisis in Greece

The economic decline of Greece was one of the most striking outcomes of the 2008 global financial crisis. Having been boosted by increased infrastructure spending and the associated benefits which resulted from hosting the Olympic Games in 2004, the Greek economy was growing by approximately 4% a year between 2002 and 2007, significantly exceeding the average growth rate seen in the euro-zone. Record levels of consumer and government spending were evidenced, financed by the increased availability of credit both individuals and institutions found available in financial markets.

Sustaining economic growth through borrowing meant Greece had established a debt–GDP ratio in excess of 100% by 2007, meaning it was hit particularly hard as a result of the credit crunch that followed. The increased cost of borrowing coupled with the greater difficulty in securing finance left the Greek economy on the verge of bankruptcy. This was avoided only by the implementation of a bail-out package from the European Central Bank exceeding €200 billion. In return for this vital injection of capital, Greece had to agree to a range of policy measures designed to reduce the size of the country's deficit, including 3% public sector wage cuts, a €500 million reduction in public investment and an increase in the two main sales tax rates.

Although the bail-out avoided the immediate threat of bankruptcy, it did not prevent significant turbulence in the Greek economy. Output contracted from €300 billion in 2010 to €227 billion in 2014, with sustained weak aggregate demand meaning the economy experienced a recession deeper and more prolonged than fellow euro-zone members. One result of this is that unemployment has remained at an unprecedentedly high level above 20% for several years, which has left millions of households struggling to afford the most basic goods and services.

Figure 1 compares changes in the unemployment rate over time in Greece with Germany, the largest economy in the euro-zone.

Table 1 illustrates the impact the crisis has had on the price index in Greece.

Consumer Price Index (2009 = 100)	
Year	Consumer Price Index
2011	108
2012	109.6
2013	108.5
2014	106.3

Table 1

While at the end of 2014 there were signs that the Greek economy was beginning to emerge from recession, a lack of confidence caused by significant uncertainty means it is likely the economy of Greece will remain fragile for some time.

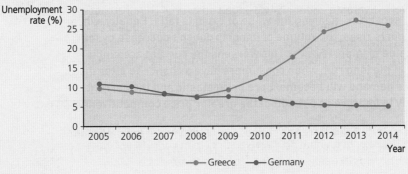

Figure 1

(a) (i) Explain what is meant by economic growth.   (2 marks)

(e) A definition of economic growth is required here, which should include reference to how it is measured.

    (ii) Using information from the case study, calculate the average annual economic growth rate in Greece between 2010 and 2014.   (3 marks)

(e) Calculate the economic growth that has occurred between 2010 and 2014, remembering you need to transform this to provide an answer which shows the annual average growth rate.

    (iii) State two examples of fiscal rules imposed on Greece by the European Central Bank.   (2 marks)

(e) Pick out two examples of fiscal rules given in the case study, quoting directly from the material provided. Because this question asks you only to 'state' them, no explanation is required.

(b) 'Unemployment has remained at an unprecedentedly high level above 20% for several years.'

    (i) State two methods of measuring unemployment.   (2 marks)

(e) This is a knowledge-recall question, which requires you to know the two methods of measuring unemployment. These do not need to be explained.

    (ii) Using Figure 1, compare the pattern of unemployment in Greece with that of Germany between 2005 and 2014.   (2 marks)

(e) At least two similarities/differences between what has happened to unemployment in Greece and Germany should be noted, with specific reference to the data in Figure 1 needed.

(c) Using Table 1, explain, with relevant calculations, whether the Greek economy is experiencing inflation in 2014.   (4 marks)

(e) First calculate the rate of inflation in 2014. Then explain whether your answer indicates that the Greek economy is experiencing inflation.

(d) 'The economy experienced a recession deeper and more prolonged than fellow euro-zone members.'

Evaluate the consequences of a recession.   (10 marks)

(e) The directive word 'Evaluate' means a two-sided answer is required here. You will need to use economic theory to explain the negative consequences of a recession on the macroeconomic policy objectives, followed by consideration of why a recession may not be harmful (or may be less harmful) than first analysed. You should then reach a supported judgement.

Student A

(a) (i) Economic growth is an increase in total output produced in an economy. It is measured by the annual percentage increase in real GDP.

---

e **2/2 marks awarded**. Candidate correctly defines economic growth. The mention of 'real' GDP is important – if nominal output is rising at a slower rate than the price level then economic growth is not occurring as real output is actually falling.

> **(ii)** Economic growth 2010–2014 = ($227bn – $300bn) ÷ $300bn × 100 = –24.3%
>
> Annual economic growth rate = –24.3% ÷ 4 = –6.08%

e **3/3 marks awarded**. Correct methodology and answer. The economic growth experienced over a four-year period is divided by 4 to calculate the average annual growth rate.

> **(iii)** A rule has been imposed by the European Central Bank to provide Greece with a €200 billion bailout. Another rule is that Greece has been forced to reduce its spending on public investment by €500 million.

e **1/2 marks awarded**. The forced reduction in public investment is a correct example of a fiscal rule. The granting of the bailout is not a rule – the bailout does not represent a restriction on future taxation or spending decisions but is a one-off payment designed to help the Greek economy.

> **(b)** **(i)** Claimant Count and Labour Force Survey.

e **2/2 marks awarded**. Candidate correctly identifies both of the methods used to measure unemployment.

> **(ii)** Between 2005 and 2008 Greece and Germany experienced a similar unemployment rate, with unemployment decreasing steadily from approximately 10% to 7%. After 2008 Greece experienced significantly rising unemployment while unemployment in Germany continued to steadily fall; this meant that by 2014 unemployment in Greece was 25% while unemployment in Germany was 5%.

e **2/2 marks awarded**. The student makes comparisons between Greece and Germany throughout the answer. A similarity is clearly identified at the start of the period, with a difference identified at the end of the period.

> **(c)** 2014 inflation rate = (106.3 – 108.5) ÷ 108.5 × 100 = **–2.03%**
>
> This means that Greece is experiencing a negative rate of inflation in 2014.

e **3/4 marks awarded**. The calculation of the inflation rate is correct, showing a strong understanding of how to use price indices to calculate inflation. However, there is no explanation of what a negative rate of inflation means – the student needs to explain that this represents deflation, which means prices in the economy are falling.

(d) A recession occurs when there are two consecutive quarters of negative economic growth. One consequence of a recession is that it is likely to result in unemployment rising. When output is falling the derived demand for labour will fall, as fewer workers will be needed to produce a lower level of output. This causes unemployment to increase.

An increase in unemployment will put pressure on the government budget. This is because the government will receive less tax revenue (no income tax is paid by those made unemployed and because these individuals experience a fall in their disposable income, spending tax receipts from these individuals also fall) and will see spending on unemployment benefits increase. This is likely to increase the budget deficit, which will add to the size of the economy's national debt – potentially having long-term damaging consequences.

However, the extent to which a recession will have these negative consequences on an economy depends upon a number of factors, the first being the length of a recession. If the economy bounces back to economic growth following two quarters of negative growth then the recession will clearly be less damaging than if it lasts for several years. The harm caused to an economy also depends on the position of the government budget prior to the recession. If the government was running a budget surplus when the economy was booming then it is more likely to be able to cope with a recession without experiencing severely damaging consequences, as the surplus built up during the boom years can be used to fund the deficit during a recession.

In conclusion, recessions are likely to harm an economy because of the lost output, increased unemployment and increased budget deficit that result. However, quite how harmful a recession is depends upon the state of government finances. If they are already fragile going into the recession, with a large budget deficit and significant national debt, the recession could be hugely problematic. Whereas if a recession occurs when the government budget is in a healthy state, it is more likely to cause a temporary decline rather than long-term damage to the economy's fortunes.

ⓔ **10/10 marks awarded**. This is a very well-structured answer. It demonstrates a clear knowledge of what a recession is, followed by strong analysis of the impact a recession can have on the macroeconomy. A clear link is made to the macroeconomic objective of low unemployment along with the long-term consequences of a recession, such as its ability to cause a debt crisis. There is strong evaluation which recognises that the duration of the recession and state of government finances are key determinants which must be known in order to measure the magnitude of the impact a recession will have on the economy. The answer finishes with a well-supported judgement which recognises that while a recession is always harmful, the extent of such harm depends upon a number of factors.

Student B

(a) (i) Economic growth is equal to GDP, which measures how many goods and services are produced in an economy.

e 1/2 marks awarded. While the student offers a correct explanation of how output is measured, the dynamic element is missing – it is only when output is *increasing* that economic growth is taking place.

(ii) Economic growth = ($300bn – $227bn) ÷ $227bn × 100 = **32.2%**. There has been negative economic growth.

e 1/3 marks awarded. The student recognises that a contraction in output means there has been negative economic growth, but the calculation is incorrect. Remember not to fall into the trap of simply subtracting the smaller number from the bigger number when calculating growth rates – if you do this you will only ever end up with a positive growth rate. You should always check your answer to see whether it makes sense given the context of the case study – given the case study is about the struggles the Greek economy has been experiencing, a growth rate in excess of 30% seems unlikely. The student here has also forgotten the average annual element of this question – the two levels of output presented here are not for two consecutive years.

(iii) Fiscal rules are designed to limit spending and increase taxation. One example is reducing the size of the deficit and another example is increasing the taxes on spending.

e 1/2 marks awarded. No marks are awarded for a definition in this question. Reducing the size of the deficit is not an example of a rule imposed but is instead the general principle behind what the rules were trying to achieve. Forcing Greece to increase taxes on spending is a correct example of a fiscal rule.

(b) (i) One measure is the International Labour Organisation unemployment rate, which is measured through a survey, and another measure is the Consumer Price Index.

e 1/2 marks awarded. The ILO (Labour Force Survey) measure is correctly identified. The student confuses measures of inflation and unemployment when mentioning the Consumer Price Index.

(ii) Unemployment in Greece increased and unemployment in Germany fell. In 2005 Greece had an unemployment rate of 10% and in 2014 the rate was 25%. In Germany unemployment was 11% in 2005 and 5% in 2014.

e 1/2 marks awarded. The correct overall trend of rising unemployment in Greece and falling unemployment in Germany is identified. However, the use of data is too descriptive – you must be careful to avoid simply repeating the data without offering any insight into what it shows. On questions such as this you should attempt to spot similarities and differences between the two datasets.

> **(c)** 2014 inflation rate = (106.3 – 108.5) = **–2.2%**
>
> Deflation is occurring in Greece as the price level is falling.

🅔 **2/4 marks awarded**. The calculation is incorrect – to calculate inflation using a price index the formula *(new index value – previous index value) ÷ previous index value x 100* must be used. You can conduct a simple calculation of *new index value – previous index value* only when the previous index value is the base year (i.e. the index in the previous year was equal to 100). The interpretation of what is happening to inflation in Greece is correct, showing a good understanding of what is meant by deflation.

> **(d)** Because a recession means less output is being produced, individuals will see their disposable income fall because they are producing less output. This means a recession will damage standard of living as individuals can afford to purchase fewer goods and services. Wages are likely to fall further as during a recession firms are likely to cut workers' wages in order to reduce costs in an attempt to survive.
>
> However, how bad a recession is depends on the size of the fall in output – if output falls by 10% there will clearly be a bigger impact on the economy than if output falls by 1%. It also depends upon which country the recession takes place in – recessions will be particularly harmful in developing economies where public finances are more fragile and falling output is likely to mean essential goods and services can no longer be afforded.
>
> Overall, recessions will harm the economy, but how much they harm the economy by depends upon a number of factors.

🅔 **5/10 marks awarded**. There is good analysis explaining how a recession leads to a fall in standard of living, but the answer would benefit from greater development linking to how a recession impacts upon the government's macroeconomic policy objectives. This could have been done through an explanation that falling wages are likely to result in the aggregate demand curve shifting to the left, which would cause further reductions in output and an increase in unemployment. The evaluation is reasonable – while the size of the fall in output is considered, this is not developed. The consideration of the impact on developing countries is interesting, but the judgement is not well supported as the student does not clearly tell us when a recession will or won't be most damaging.

∎ AS macroeconomics Section C

Essay questions

Question 1

In July 2012, the Bank of England's Monetary Policy Committee decided to purchase £50 billion of additional assets, bringing total spending on quantitative easing to £375 billion since 2009.

Evaluate, using an appropriate diagram(s), the effectiveness of using quantitative easing to achieve the government's macroeconomic objectives.   (20 marks)

ⓔ The answer must start with an explanation of what quantitative easing is and an analysis of how it can be used to achieve the government's macroeconomic objectives. An *AD/AS* diagram should be used to illustrate this and referred to in the analysis. The limitations of the policy must then be considered before reaching a judgement on the effectiveness of quantitative easing, which should include recognition of the circumstances under which it will be most/least effective.

Student A

Quantitative easing (QE) is a desirable policy tool to ensure inflation does not fall below target when cutting interest rates is no longer possible because nominal interest rates are close to zero. ⓐ By purchasing financial assets from firms, banks and insurers, the Bank of England is essentially increasing the supply of money in the economy by electronically creating money. Because the balance sheets of financial institutions are now boosted by this additional money supply, this should make them more willing to lend to earn a return on this money. This increase in the supply of lending should lower the interest rate and, crucially, increase the availability of credit at a time when it is hard to come by. ⓑ

An increase in the availability and decrease in the cost of borrowing should increase consumption and investment. When it is easier and cheaper to borrow, firms will enjoy a better return from their investment so investment will rise. Consumers also now have access to borrowing they didn't have before, meaning they can now afford to purchase more goods and services. ⓒ As consumption and investment are both components of aggregate demand, an increase in consumption and investment will cause the aggregate demand curve to shift to the right from AD_1 to AD_2, as illustrated on the next page.

This will cause the price level to increase from P_1 to P_2, avoiding deflationary pressures and ensuring the price level rises in line with the inflation target of 2%. There is the additional benefit of real output increasing from Y_1 to Y_2, meaning economic growth is boosted. Unemployment is also likely to fall, as the derived demand for labour will increase. ⓓ Overall, QE will therefore be very effective in achieving the government's macroeconomic objectives.

However, QE will be ineffective when there is a significant level of spare capacity in the economy. This is because any increases in aggregate demand under such

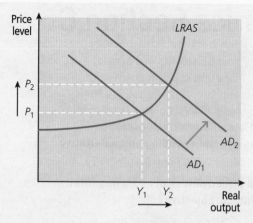

circumstances will not lead to any increase in the price level, as illustrated in the figure below. e

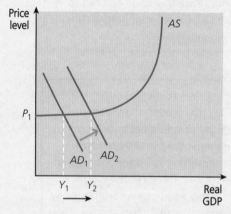

There is also a danger that QE will fail to achieve the 2% inflation target because there are many other factors which affect inflation. Rising commodity prices during the period QE was implemented in the UK meant that inflation exceeded the 2% target, peaking at 5% in 2011. f

Moreover, some question the effectiveness of the transmission mechanism QE requires to be successful. While it certainly does improve the balance sheets of banks, it can be argued that financial institutions have become more risk averse so have simply used this extra money supply to increase their cash holdings, rather than increase lending. g This means the availability of credit has not increased as rapidly as hoped and limits the effectiveness of QE.

In conclusion, QE is likely to be effective in achieving the inflation target because it provides another route to influence aggregate demand when nominal interest rates are already close to zero. Its ability to increase the availability of credit at a time when credit is in short supply is also desirable in helping the macroeconomy recover from a recession. However, it should be recognised that not all money spent on QE is likely to filter through to the real economy; how much of it does depends upon the attitude of financial institutions to lending, meaning business confidence is important in determining the policy's effectiveness. h

ⓔ 19/20 marks awarded. ⓐ The student begins by recognising the primary purpose of quantitative easing and understanding that it is most likely to be used when interest rate changes are rendered ineffective because of the liquidity trap. ⓑ This is followed by a clear explanation of how QE results in a greater supply of credit and lower interest rates. ⓒ The monetary policy transmission mechanism is then detailed to explain how this results in an increase in aggregate demand. ⓓ An accurate diagram is drawn and strong analysis of this is offered by the student, with excellent links back to the government's macroeconomic objectives. ⓔ The evaluation is strong, recognising that QE will be ineffective when there is significant spare capacity. The student could have mentioned at this point that, given that QE is often implemented during a recession, the fact that QE is ineffective under such circumstances is particularly relevant. ⓕ Excellent contextual understanding is shown when reference is made to the high inflation seen following QE in the UK as a result of cost-push pressures. ⓖ The weaknesses of the transmission mechanism are also illustrated, questioning the extent to which QE actually results in an increased availability of credit. ⓗ A strong supported judgement is reached, with clear conditions set out which determine the circumstances under which QE will be most effective.

Student B

Implementing a policy of quantitative easing (QE) serves to increase the money supply and stimulate the economy at a time of sluggish or negative economic growth. By reducing the cost of borrowing, it will make individuals and firms borrow more, resulting in an increase in aggregate demand in the economy and causing the aggregate demand curve to shift to the right from AD_1 to AD_2 as illustrated below. ⓐ

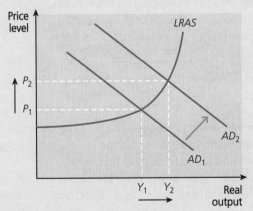

This results in an increase in real output from Y_1 to Y_2, meaning the policy is effective in stimulating economic growth. This was a primary factor motivating the implementation of QE in 2009 and it is thought to have helped the UK economy avoid experiencing a deeper and more prolonged recession. ⓑ Unemployment will also decrease as unemployment is positively correlated with economic growth. ⓒ

However, one of the disadvantages of QE is that it results in inflation, with the price level increasing from P_1 to P_2. ⓓ Moreover, the fact that money supply in the economy has increased generates potential for further inflation in the future, which could harm the macroeconomy. Some also argue that policies designed to promote more available and cheaper borrowing in this way could just incentivise more irresponsible lending to individuals who are not credit-worthy – this could be considered disadvantageous as it was an overly buoyant credit market which led to the financial crisis in the first place. e

Overall, QE is likely to be effective in stimulating economic growth, but this could come at the cost of higher inflation and potentially create a boom in lending which could cause problems in the long term. f

e 11/20 marks awarded. a The student offers good analysis, which explains that QE results in the aggregate demand curve shifting to the right because of a decrease in the cost of borrowing, but some links in this explanation are missing. Explaining how QE results in a decrease in the cost of borrowing would strengthen the answer, while the student should also link to the aggregate demand equation to explain why increases in consumption and investment increase aggregate demand. b There is a good analysis of how an increase in aggregate demand results in economic growth occurring, thus demonstrating a key benefit of QE. c Reference to the reduction in unemployment that results from economic growth demonstrates a further benefit of QE. d When evaluating, while recognising that QE can result in an increase in the price level, the student incorrectly assumes this to be a bad thing. In reality, QE is often implemented when there is a danger of deflation, meaning the rising price level which QE causes is actually a desired outcome of the policy. e There is, however, good evaluation offered about the long-term problems associated with the policy of QE, particularly when analysing the dangers of promoting growth in consumption financed by cheaper borrowing as the way out of a recession. f The judgement reached offers a solid conclusion to the preceding analysis, but again highlights the main weakness of this answer, which is its failure to recognise QE as a monetary policy implemented by the MPC, which, ultimately, is responsible for achieving the inflation target.

Question 2

During the 2010 election campaign, the Conservative Party pledged to decrease net migration to below 100,000 in the next parliament. In 2015 opposition leaders claimed Prime Minister David Cameron had failed to achieve this, with net migration exceeding 250,000. Evaluate, using an appropriate diagram(s), whether UK macroeconomic performance would be strengthened by a reduction in immigration.

(20 marks)

e The answer should begin with an analysis outlining the reasons why reducing immigration might help achieve the government's macroeconomic objectives. An *AD/AS* diagram should be used to illustrate this and should be referred to during the analysis. Evaluation should consider the potential benefits of immigration and how reducing immigration may not achieve desirable outcomes in terms of the macroeconomic policy objectives. Finally, a judgement should be reached clearly stating whether a reduction in immigration will or will not improve macroeconomic performance, supported by a relevant argument.

Student A

A reduction in immigration could result in an increase in wage rates. When there is a decrease in the supply of labour as net migration falls, the wage rate will increase. This increases individuals' real disposable income, meaning they can afford to purchase more goods and services, and causes consumption to increase. As consumption is a component of aggregate demand ($AD = C + I + G + X - M$), an increase in consumption will cause the aggregate demand curve to shift to the right as illustrated below from AD_1 to AD_2. [a]

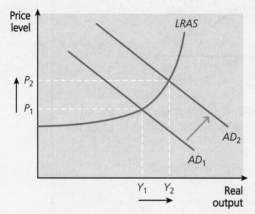

This will generate economic growth, with real output increasing from Y_1 to Y_2. [b] Moreover, reduced immigration will help ease the housing crisis in Britain. A limited supply of housing coupled with ever increasing demand has made it increasingly difficult for individuals to find affordable housing, which has created a number of problems. A decrease in immigration will reduce the demand for housing. This should reduce the cost of buying/renting a house, leaving individuals with more disposable income to spend on goods and services, causing further increases in consumption and aggregate demand. [c]

However, it could be argued that macroeconomic performance could be weakened as a result of immigration falling. Firstly, a decrease in immigration may cause aggregate demand to fall as there are fewer individuals demanding goods and services in the economy. More significantly, a reduction in immigration will reduce the economy's productive capacity. Given most immigrants tend to be of working age, a reduction in immigration will result in the aggregate supply curve shifting to the left, as the size of the labour force will decrease. As illustrated in the figure below, a shift of aggregate demand to the left from AD_1 to AD_2 alongside an inward shift of the aggregate supply curve from AS_1 to AS_2 could result in a significant reduction in real output, from Y_1 to Y_2. [d]

During boom periods the UK economy has relied on immigration to provide the additional labour supply needed to fuel economic growth; this reduction in the economy's productive capacity could limit the potential for the economy to grow in the future. [e] In particular, immigration often helps to fill skills shortages in the domestic economy. For example, many of the extra nurses the NHS has required have been immigrants. A reduction in immigration could leave jobs in

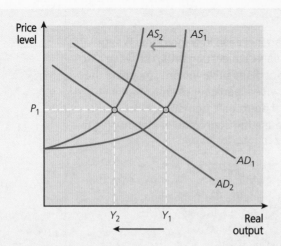

which there are domestic skills shortages unfilled, limiting economic growth and potentially causing problems in the provision of public services such as the NHS which rely on immigrant workers. f

In judgement, reducing immigration is unlikely to strengthen UK macroeconomic performance in the long term, as it will reduce the productive capacity of the economy and therefore limit future growth. However, whether it improves performance in the short term depends upon the current state of the macroeconomy. If there is significant spare capacity and high levels of unemployment, reducing immigration is likely to be beneficial. g

e **17/20 marks awarded**. a There is a strong analysis of how reduced immigration will increase wages and subsequently increase the level of aggregate demand in the economy. b The positive impact this would have on economic growth is well explained and supported by an accurate diagram. Consideration of the impact this has on unemployment would strengthen the analysis, particularly given unemployment is such an important element of the immigration debate. c The student recognises that reduced immigration will help overcome the housing shortage and offers a developed explanation of how this will improve macroeconomic performance. d Strong evaluation is offered, explaining how falling immigration could cause a reduction in real output as the productive capacity of the economy shrinks. However, the student should recognise that a reduction in immigration doesn't necessarily mean the aggregate supply curve will shift inwards – providing net migration is still positive it simply means the aggregate supply curve will shift out at a slower rate. e The historical context of the benefits of immigration is well explained. f There is strong evaluation of the way in which a reduction in immigration could worsen the problems associated with skills shortages. g The judgement cleverly explains how the impact of reducing immigration may differ in the short term and the long term, but a final piece of analysis is needed explaining how, when significant spare capacity exists, reducing immigration is advantageous because it simply reduces the level of unemployment without harming real output.

Student B

One of the harms of immigration is that it displaces domestic workers. Given the UK is one of the world's richest economies, immigrants are often prepared to enter the labour market and work for lower wages than domestic workers, as these wages are higher than they would be able to earn in their home country. This makes it difficult for domestic workers in certain industries, such as construction, to find employment, as they are more expensive than immigrant workers. Decreasing immigration will free up jobs for domestic workers, decreasing unemployment. a

Immigration is also thought to put strain on public services, such as education and healthcare, as well as on some welfare benefits. Reducing immigration will reduce the pressure on these services and could help reduce government spending on these areas. b

Falling immigration could be seen to harm the economy because it will increase the dependency ratio. The UK population is ageing, meaning immigration is needed to ensure there are enough workers to support the retired population. As illustrated below, immigration can help increase potential and actual output as it increases the quantity of labour – these benefits are lost if immigration is reduced. c

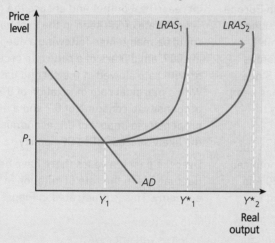

It could also be argued that reducing immigration will harm the flexibility of the labour market. Immigrant workers tend to be more geographically and occupationally mobile; having fewer immigrants in the workforce could therefore reduce the flexibility of the labour market and thus the economy. d

Ultimately, reducing immigration will help reduce unemployment and cut government spending on welfare benefits. This is particularly true if the government targets reducing individuals who are outside of the labour market from immigrating. e

e 14/20 marks awarded. a A good analysis is offered of how decreasing immigration may help to reduce domestic unemployment. b The potential decrease in government spending on public services is well explained. However, the answer would benefit from more technical detail; the analysis should offer a diagrammatic

explanation of how falling immigration may improve macroeconomic performance.
c There is good evaluation of the damage falling immigration could do to the
economy in terms of increasing the dependency ratio. d The student further
recognises the damage falling immigration could do to labour market flexibility,
but this evaluative point would be stronger if the reasons why immigrant workers
are more geographically and occupationally mobile were explained. e The answer
reaches a valid conclusion which could be better developed – presumably the
student is suggesting that reforming the immigration policy so only immigrants
who intend to participate in the labour market enter the country will be most
beneficial as this will provide the least drain on public finances.

■ A-level macroeconomics Section A

Data response

Estonian tax reform

In 1994, Estonia became the first country in Europe
to adopt a flat tax rate on income tax, replacing
three different tax rates on personal income
with a single rate. Those on the lowest incomes
were exempt from paying any income tax. Since
implementing this regime the rate of tax has been
cut a number of times as part of a strategy to
become a low-tax economy.

In 2004, the Estonian government decided to cut
its tax rate from 26% to 24%. In 2013 it announced
plans to reduce the rate of income tax to 20% in
2015. This €55 million tax cut was designed to
increase real output and ensure the economic
growth rate of 3% seen in the first half of 2013
could be maintained following a deep recession
in 2009, amid fears of a return to recession as the
growth rate slowed in the second half of the year.
With a marginal rate of taxation of 0.2, a marginal
propensity to consume of 0.7 and a marginal
propensity to import of 0.1, economists questioned
the likely success of such a policy.

Over the past ten years there have been significant
fluctuations in the rate of inflation in the Estonian
economy. This is illustrated in Figure 1.

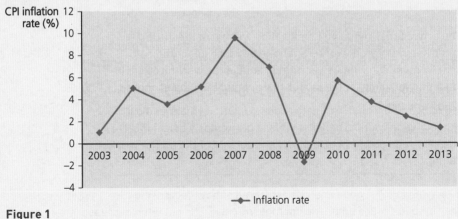

Figure 1

Having dismantled many of the trade barriers of the Soviet era when returning to independence in 1991, Estonia became one of the world's most free trading nations, which initially helped to generate a strong surplus on the current account. However, in recent years the balance of trade in goods and services has been persistently negative, as illustrated in Figure 2. Joining the euro in January 2011 and continuing to reduce tax rates were part of a coordinated strategy to encourage foreign investment in an attempt to offset this poor trading performance.

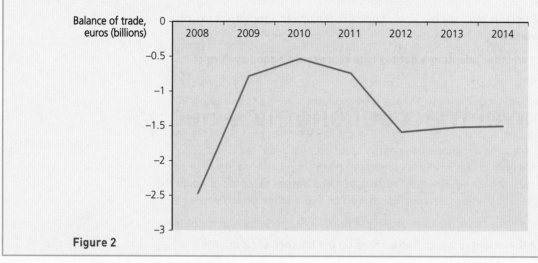

Figure 2

(a) Using information from the case study, calculate by how much national income is expected to increase as a result of the Estonian government's 2015 income tax cut.

(3 marks)

ⓔ Calculate the size of the multiplier effect and use this to calculate the impact the tax cut will have on national income/total output.

(b) 'In 2004, the Estonian government decided to cut its tax rate from 26% to 24%.'

Using evidence from the case study, explain **one** possible policy conflict that may have resulted from this decision to cut taxes.

(2 marks)

ⓔ Start by identifying the policy conflict between two macroeconomic policy objectives that is likely to result from the decision to cut taxes and then present evidence from the case study that demonstrates this conflict occurred in Estonia.

(c) Using Figure 1, explain what was happening to the price level in Estonia between 2007 and 2009.

(2 marks)

ⓔ This question requires you to explain two features or patterns of changes in the price level over the period shown, quoting the data to provide support for each point.

(d) Using Figure 2, explain whether it is true to say that Estonia's balance of trade in goods and services went from a deficit to a surplus between 2008 and 2010.   (3 marks)

ⓔ Begin by stating whether the statement is true or false. If it is true, use data to explain why. If it is not true, you need to provide the correct explanation of what happened to Estonia's balance of trade and offer evidence to support this explanation.

(e) 'In 1994, Estonia became the first country in Europe to adopt a flat tax rate on income tax.'

Evaluate whether adopting a flat tax rate represents a good system of taxation.   (8 marks)

ⓔ The directive word 'Evaluate' means a two-sided answer is required here. You should begin by analysing why a flat tax rate system may represent a good system of taxation, using any features of a 'good' tax which apply here. This should be followed by a consideration of any of the features of a 'good' tax which a flat tax system does not offer. Finally, a judgement needs to be offered in which you reach a conclusion over whether the advantages of a flat tax system outweigh the disadvantages, supporting this conclusion with an explanation of why you have come to this decision.

(f) Evaluate the extent to which imbalances on the balance of payments are harmful to an economy.   (12 marks)

ⓔ The directive word 'Evaluate' means a two-sided answer is required here. Begin by offering detailed economic analysis of why imbalances may harm an economy, remembering to refer to the macroeconomic policy objectives. Then consider circumstances in which imbalances would not be particularly harmful, supporting these points with a thorough explanation. Finally reach a supported judgement which justifies whether imbalances on the balance of payments are harmful to an economy.

Student A

(a) The size of the multiplier can be calculated by 1 ÷ marginal propensity to withdraw.

$MPW = 0.2 + 0.3 + 0.1 = 0.6$

Multiplier $= 1 ÷ 0.6 = 1.67$

So a €55 million tax cut should result in an increase in output of:

55 million × 1.67 = **€91.85 million**

ⓔ **3/3 marks awarded.** Candidate correctly calculates the multiplier effect. However, they should have stated the equation for the marginal propensity to withdraw so the examiner could have awarded marks for their workings if they had made a mistake with the calculation. The multiplier is then correctly applied to calculate the impact on national income of the tax cut.

(b) As shown in Figure 1, the tax cut has resulted in high inflation – after the tax rate was cut in 2004 the rate of inflation increased from 4% to nearly 10% in the subsequent years.

e **1/2 marks awarded**. The student has recognised that increasing taxes has led to higher inflation and has used appropriate evidence from the case study to support this. However, they have not clearly identified the policy conflict – that a policy designed to achieve economic growth has the result of harming price stability.

(c) The price level was rising throughout most of the period, but the rate at which the price level was increasing was decreasing. In 2007 prices were increasing by nearly 10% while in 2008 prices were increasing by approximately 7%. The only year in which the price level was falling was in 2009.

e **2/2 marks awarded**. The student has recognised that a falling rate of inflation does not mean that the price level is falling and also spots the year in which the price level was falling. The answer would be even stronger if they explained that the falling price level in 2009 represents a period of deflation.

(d) It is incorrect to say the balance of trade in goods and services went from a deficit to a surplus because there was a deficit in both years, as the balance of trade was below zero. Between 2008 and 2010 the size of the deficit has fallen from –€2.5 billion to –€0.5 billion.

e **3/3 marks awarded**. A very clear answer which shows a good understanding of the meaning of a balance of trade deficit and surplus and uses the data correctly to support the explanation.

(e) A flat tax represents a good system of taxation because it delivers many of the features of a 'good' tax. For example, it meets the principle of 'economy'. A flat tax will be cheap to collect because of its uncomplicated nature – less money will need to be spent administering a system in which there are no variations in the proportion of income taken from individuals. This is efficient as it means the majority of the tax revenue can be used effectively by the government, with very little of the revenue needing to be used to operate the tax system.

The flat tax also meets the principle of 'certainty'. Many individuals get confused by complex taxes with various levels and exemptions, meaning they find it difficult to predict how much of their income will be taxed. This creates a degree of uncertainty which could limit spending. A flat tax system means all individuals will be able to clearly understand the amount of tax they will have to pay, giving them more confidence when budgeting on how to spend the rest of their income.

However, the problem of a flat tax system is that it goes against the important principle of 'equity'. A fundamental purpose of the taxation system is to redistribute incomes. A flat tax loses the progressive nature of many income tax systems, meaning all individuals pay the same proportion of their income. This seems unfair because it does not account for the fact that individuals on higher incomes are likely to be more easily able to afford to pay a higher proportion of their income on taxation.

In conclusion, a flat tax system does seem to be advantageous, largely because it simplifies what in many countries is an overly complicated and rarely understood system of taxation. However, it is only good providing it has an element of fairness by providing a tax exemption for those on low incomes.

ⓔ **6/8 marks awarded**. The answer offers a strong analysis of the advantages of a flat tax system, which are well linked to the features of a 'good' tax. It is perhaps unusual though that the incentive effects for high earners are not mentioned. The evaluation recognises that not all features of a 'good' tax system are fulfilled by a flat tax. The supported judgement concludes that flat taxes are ultimately advantageous because of their simplicity. The conditions attached to the judgement could have been further developed. For example, the student could have mentioned that the conclusion that a flat tax system is preferable holds only if it can be implemented without an overall reduction in the tax take; this is crucial for the implementation of such a regime to be feasible.

(f) Large trade deficits as seen in Estonia can be harmful to an economy. A trade deficit means net exports are negative. As net exports are a component of aggregate demand ($AD = C + I + G + X - M$), an increasing trade deficit will cause the aggregate demand curve to shift to the left from AD_1 to AD_2, as illustrated below.

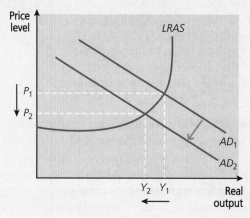

This could result in a fall in real output and therefore means a trade deficit has the potential to cause a recession. It also results in there being significant spare capacity in the economy; because domestic products are not highly demanded by foreign consumers, it creates a negative output gap and is likely to lead to unemployment, with domestic firms laying off workers because of a lack of demand for their products.

However, the extent to which imbalances are harmful depends upon the state of the economy. In instances where aggregate demand is rising rapidly in the economy and the economy is in danger of over-heating, a trade deficit can actually be beneficial in reducing inflationary pressures. When real incomes rise, demand for imports increases, causing aggregate demand to shift to the left as shown in the previous figure. This will result in the price level falling, reducing inflationary pressures. Moreover, the harm imbalances cause depends upon the size of the trade deficit as a percentage of GDP. If the trade deficit only accounts for a small percentage of GDP, perhaps because international trade is a relatively insignificant part of the economy, it is unlikely to cause significant damage to macroeconomic performance.

Ultimately, imbalances on the balance of payments harm an economy because of the negative impact they have on aggregate demand and, therefore, the damage they can do to economic growth and unemployment. Whether this is the case though does depend on the cause of the trade deficit, as it is most problematic when caused by uncompetitive exports.

ⓔ **10/12 marks awarded**. There is strong analysis of the harm a trade deficit can do to an economy, with good use of the *AD/AS* model to link to the macroeconomic objectives of economic growth and full employment. The evaluation is excellent as it explains a number of circumstances which determine the significance of the trade deficit. The explanation that a trade deficit can help to reduce inflationary pressures could be developed by recognising that this is most relevant when the economy is operating close to full capacity, as this is when inflationary pressures are most severe. There is a clear supported judgement which could be further extended by explaining that, when there is a trade deficit simply because there is a large volume of imports because of high incomes (rather than because there is a low volume of exports because they are uncompetitive), the trade deficit is unlikely to be harmful to an economy.

Student B

(a) The multiplier $= 1 - MPT - MPS - MPM$

$= 1 - 0.2 - 0.3 - 0.1 = 0.4$

So a €55 million tax cut should result in an increase in output of:

55 million $\times$ 0.4 = **€22 million**

ⓔ **1/3 marks awarded.** The multiplier equation used is incorrect – the student has correctly calculated the marginal propensity to withdraw but has interpreted the multiplier as being 1 minus the marginal propensity to withdraw rather than 1 divided by the marginal propensity to withdraw. The student has correctly identified that they need to multiply the multiplier by the size of the tax cut to find the change in national income, but having an incorrect multiplier means they arrive at the incorrect final answer.

> **(b)** There is a trade-off between pursuing economic growth and low inflation, as while cutting taxes leads to an increase in aggregate demand and therefore causes output to increase, it also results in demand-pull inflation.

ⓔ **1/2 marks awarded.** A strong technical answer which lacks application to the case study – evidence needs to be provided to demonstrate that this policy conflict is not only theoretical but can be seen in the case of Estonia.

> **(c)** Between 2003 and 2007 the price level was rising, from 1% to 10%. The price level then fell from 10% to –1% before increasing again after 2009.

ⓔ **0/2 marks awarded.** The data have been interpreted incorrectly here – in all the years in which the rate of inflation is above zero the price level is not falling but rising; the downward slope of the curve simply represents that prices are rising at a slower rate. It is very important to read the question carefully – reference to the period 2003–07 could not be awarded any marks even if the analysis was valid because it is outside the scope of the question asked.

> **(d)** No, because there is a deficit in both years. The deficit is –€2.5 billion in 2008 and –€0.5 billion in 2010.

ⓔ **1/3 marks awarded.** While there is recognition that the statement is incorrect, the correct description for what is happening during the period has not been given – the data are provided but an interpretation of what this shows needs to be offered.

> **(e)** Flat taxes are an unfair system of taxation because they go against the government's macroeconomic objective of improving the distribution of income. This is because charging everyone the same percentage of their income regardless of their income level means those on low incomes end up paying more tax than they would if a standard tax system were in place where the rich bear a higher burden.
>
> However, the one advantage of a flat tax system is that it provides an incentive to work as individuals are giving a lower proportion of their income to the government, meaning they get to keep more of any extra income they earn. This may encourage individuals to work more hours, increasing output in the economy.

ⓔ **4/8 marks awarded**. This is a reasonable attempt at a two-sided discussion. The analysis describes the unfairness associated with flat taxes but would benefit from being more technical – reference to progressive or proportional tax systems is needed and a link to the features of a 'good' tax would strengthen the answer. The student then recognises there is a positive incentives effect of a flat rate of tax, but this is not well explained – this incentive effect occurs only for those on high incomes, as it is only those who previously earned in the higher tax bracket which is abolished under a flat tax system who keep a higher proportion of their disposable income. The answer is lacking a judgement – it is crucial to reach a reasoned conclusion in your argument that explains which side of the debate you think is stronger.

> **(f)** Imbalances on the balance of payments are harmful because they could lead to a debt crisis. If there is a trade deficit this will be paid for by borrowing from other countries. When this happens over a long period of time the country can essentially be said to be living beyond its means. This, alongside a likely depreciation in the currency resulting from the high demand for foreign currency, is likely to lead to foreign investors losing confidence, resulting in capital outflows which could further harm the economy.
>
> However, it could be argued that a trade deficit is a sign of strength, as it suggests there is a high value of imports. Given imports have a positive income elasticity of demand, this may suggest the economy is experiencing rising income. In the short term, this is likely to benefit individuals' material standards, as they will enjoy the consumption of more luxury goods and services (imports are often luxury goods). Moreover, imbalances on the balance of payments are not necessarily a problem but are an inevitability – some countries will have good balances on areas of strength and negative balances on areas of weakness.

ⓔ **7/12 marks awarded**. There is good analysis of how persistent trade deficits can lead to excessive foreign debt. However, the student needs to make links to the harm this excessive foreign debt can cause to the government's macroeconomic objectives – for example, reduced confidence could cause the aggregate demand curve to shift to the left and harm economic growth and unemployment. The evaluation is reasonable as it identifies situations in which balance of payments imbalances are not problematic, but it doesn't interact with the 'extent to which' element of the question – there needs to be a discussion explaining when imbalances are most harmful. The final point about imbalances being an inevitability is poorly phrased – a clearer explanation is required detailing that a current account deficit, for example, is not necessarily problematic to some economies which are structured in a way in which their capital account is positive. Finally, the answer is missing a supported judgement.

■ A-level macroeconomics Section B

Quantitative essay question

China's exchange rate is closely controlled by government authorities, with the People's Bank of China (PBoC) managing the value of the yuan by fixing its price against the US dollar. For many years, the yuan has been deliberately undervalued by the PBoC.

Evaluate, using an appropriate diagram(s), the extent to which undervaluing the exchange rate in this way will improve macroeconomic performance.

(25 marks)

(e) The answer should begin with an analysis which details how undervaluing the exchange rate can improve macroeconomic performance, using the *AD/AS* model to link back to the government's macroeconomic objectives. Consideration should be given to the harm undervaluation can do to macroeconomic performance before moving on to evaluate the circumstances under which undervaluation will be most/least desirable. The answer should conclude by reaching a supported judgement justifying whether or not you believe undervaluing the exchange rate has a beneficial impact on macroeconomic performance.

Student A

Undervaluing the exchange rate means the Chinese yuan is kept artificially 'cheap'. This means that one unit of a foreign currency can be exchanged for a lot of yuan and that the yuan cannot be exchanged for much foreign currency. This effectively increases the price competitiveness of domestically produced products, as less foreign currency has to be exchanged for the domestic product, increasing the demand for exports. Moreover, it worsens the price competitiveness of imports, as domestic consumers have to swap more of their currency to purchase foreign goods and services. The result of this is that exports rise and imports fall, increasing net exports. (a) As net exports is a component of aggregate demand $(AD = C + I + G + X - M)$, an increase in net exports will cause the aggregate demand curve to shift to the right, as illustrated below. (b)

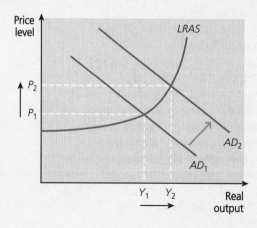

The result is that real output increases from Y_1 to Y_2, meaning undervaluing the exchange rate is effective in achieving economic growth. In fact, keeping the exchange rate competitive has been a key strategy for China to maintain its high growth levels, with a consistent focus on export-led growth. Moreover, unemployment is likely to be low as a consequence of this undervaluation. This is because the derived demand for labour is high – there is a lot of demand for domestically produced goods and services from both domestic and foreign consumers, meaning more workers are needed to produce this high level of output. c

However, the J-curve effect illustrates how depreciating the value of the currency to keep it undervalued may not improve macroeconomic performance. This is because in the short run the volume of exports and imports may stay the same, meaning the current account is worsened. Because the price of exports has fallen and the price of imports has risen, when the quantities are unchanged this would result in the value of exports falling and the value of imports rising. This worsening of the current account is illustrated at point A on the figure below, when the depreciation takes place. d It is only in the long run, when the price elasticity of demand for imports and exports becomes more elastic, that the benefits of an undervalued exchange rate will be seen. Therefore, the impact of undervaluing the exchange rate on macroeconomic performance depends on whether the Marshall–Lerner condition holds. e

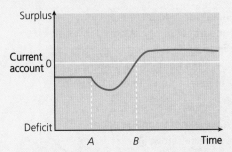

Moreover, whether undervaluing the exchange rate improves macroeconomic performance depends upon whether domestic firms rely on foreign producers for inputs in the production process. If there are a lot of imported inputs then an undervalued exchange rate will increase the price of these inputs, raising costs of production and therefore raising the price of the domestically produced products, which could offset any effect of the weak exchange rate making it cheap to purchase domestic products. f Finally, it should be recognised that this sort of policy can worsen the standard of living of domestic consumers, who cannot afford foreign imports and find domestic producers neglecting their preferences in a desire to appeal to a wealthy international market. g

To conclude, undervaluing the exchange rate will ultimately be beneficial for macroeconomic performance, as the high level of demand it generates for domestically produced products fuels economic growth and keeps unemployment low. However, ultimately this is only true when there is significant spare capacity in the economy; in recent years China has found that rising aggregate demand when approaching a capacity constraint means the policy does not achieve economic growth but is simply inflationary. h

ⓔ 21/25 marks awarded. **ⓐ** The answer demonstrates strong knowledge of how the value of an exchange rate determines international competitiveness, with a clear explanation that an undervalued exchange rate will improve net exports. **ⓑ** This is then linked to aggregate demand, with an accurate diagram illustrating the aggregate demand curve shifting to the right. **ⓒ** The analysis of this figure is excellent, demonstrating that undervaluing the exchange rate can be effective in improving macroeconomic performance in terms of achieving economic growth and low unemployment. **ⓓ** The student recognises that undervaluing the currency could worsen the current account in the short run, but would have benefited from explaining why demand for imports and exports may be inelastic in the short run. **ⓔ** Reference to the Marshall–Lerner condition is impressive but it needs explaining. **ⓕ** There is strong evaluation present, including a well-made point that undervaluing the currency is counterproductive if domestic firms rely on foreign inputs. **ⓖ** Understanding that undervaluation can harm domestic consumers demonstrates that the student is aware that such a policy might result in better outcomes on a national than an individual level. **ⓗ** The judgement reaches a clear conclusion and the reference to recent developments in China provides good evidence for this conclusion. However, a diagram illustrating this point would have added technical rigour to the judgement.

Student B

Managing the exchange rate in this way is beneficial for a country's macroeconomic performance as it helps to reduce uncertainty. When domestic and foreign firms know that the central bank is managing the exchange rate to ensure it remains undervalued, they know there is less likely to be significant fluctuations, which could affect the profitability of investment. This is likely to increase the level of investment which takes place. **ⓐ**

Undervaluing the exchange rate is likely to increase exports and reduce imports, which increases aggregate demand as shown below. **ⓑ**

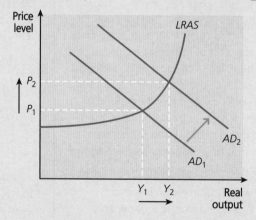

This results in output increasing from Y_1 to Y_2, meaning economic growth occurs. **ⓒ** Moreover, as exports have increased and imports have decreased the balance of payments will have improved, which is one of the government's macroeconomic objectives. **ⓓ**

However, undervaluing the exchange rate could be seen to harm macroeconomic performance in the long run, as it only artificially improves competitiveness. Domestic goods and services are only attractive because they are kept artificially cheap because of the undervalued exchange rate. This means domestic firms may not be as innovative and efficient as they could be knowing they are being given an unfair advantage in the global market. This could damage the underlying competitiveness of domestic products, which could harm the economy in the long run. e

Also, pursuing export-led growth by undervaluing the exchange rate means the domestic economy is heavily reliant on foreign demand. This increases the risk of contagion, as if foreign countries go into recession the domestic country will also be harmed, as there will be a significant reduction in aggregate demand. f

e **12/25 marks awarded.** a The student offers a good explanation of how uncertainty can be reduced as a result of managing the exchange rate. b There is recognition that undervaluing the exchange rate can result in aggregate demand increasing, but this is not well explained – there is no link to the increased price competitiveness which results from the currency being undervalued. c An accurate figure is presented with good analysis of the economic growth which results from this, but it is surprising there is no mention of the associated reduction in unemployment. d The analysis of the balance of payments is incorrect – the government targets a satisfactory balance of payments position, meaning macroeconomic performance is not necessarily improved as a result of undervaluing the currency if there was already a big trade surplus. e The evaluation is reasonable; the point about artificial competitiveness is well made and could be extended by recognising that if it does stunt development, the only way these firms will be able to compete in the future is by continued government manipulation of the exchange rate. f There is a good explanation that a country may become vulnerable to external shocks, but ultimately the answer is missing clear evaluation which considers the circumstances under which undervaluation is most/least beneficial and also fails to reach a supported judgement.

■ A-level macroeconomics Section C

Essay question

One of the 1997 Labour government's 'golden rules' of fiscal policy was that national debt should not exceed 40% of GDP. In 2015, national debt in the UK exceeded £1.4 trillion, representing approximately 78% of GDP.

Evaluate the extent to which national debt on this scale is harmful to a country's macroeconomic performance.

(25 marks)

ⓔ The answer should begin with an analysis detailing how high national debt harms a country's macroeconomic performance, with links to the government's macroeconomic objectives. Evaluation should then be offered considering how national debt is not necessarily particularly harmful to an economy and the circumstances under which debt is most damaging. The answer should finish by reaching a clear supported judgement justifying whether national debt is ultimately harmful to a country's macroeconomic performance.

Student A

One of the major problems of high levels of national debt is the damage it can do to confidence in the economy. When the national debt is very high some uncertainty starts to exist amongst consumers and firms, as high debt signals potential problems in the future. ⓐ Such uncertainty could result in consumers and firms behaving more cautiously, reducing consumption and investment. This will depress the level of aggregate demand in the economy and could harm economic growth, potentially causing the economy to slip into recession. This could create a dangerous spiral effect, as when the economy enters recession tax revenue will fall and automatic stabilisers are likely to increase government spending, which would further increase the size of the national debt. This would then damage confidence still further, trapping the economy in a negative cycle difficult to break. ⓑ

Another problem with excessive national debt is the inter-generational inequality which is likely to result. Rising national debt means the current generation is living beyond its means. Future generations will bear the burden of this debt, either in the form of paying higher taxes or enjoying fewer public services. This makes national debt undesirable as it suggests the economy is operating unsustainably. ⓒ

Rising national debt also means debt interest payments will be rising, creating significant opportunity cost. The government may be forced to cut back on spending elsewhere to finance this debt or, if committed to maintaining public services at their current level, may be forced to increase taxes, meaning individuals' real disposable income falls in order to be able to finance the national debt. The only alternative to this would be for the government to raise borrowing to pay the debt interest, which would further increase the size of the national debt and would therefore not address the underlying problem. ⓓ

However, the extent to which national debt damages the macroeconomy clearly depends upon the size of national debt compared to GDP. It could be argued that the UK's national debt level is not high enough to cause the crises of confidence outlined in the analysis as it does not suggest debt is unsustainable; for that to happen, debt would have to be much higher (perhaps closer to 200% of GDP, as seen in other nations which have been more affected by the size of their national debt). In fact, there is evidence in UK economic history that it is more than possible for an economy to cope with high levels of national debt – in the 1950s national debt exceeded 200% of GDP, and yet there was no default and the government was able to successfully increase spending to implement the NHS. e

Moreover, the extent to which a high level of national debt is harmful depends upon the interest rate charged on financing this debt. Given interest rates are at historic lows, it could be argued that national debt is not generating the large opportunity cost suggested in the analysis, as even large sums of debt do not generate as significant debt interest payments as a proportion of GDP as seen in the past because of the low interest rates being charged. Clearly, higher interest rates would make the debt problem more problematic. f Finally, the argument could be made that rising national debt is not a problem if it is helping to fuel economic growth – if GDP is rising then rising national debt is not necessarily a problem, as providing it is rising at a slower rate than the economy is growing at then national debt as a percentage of GDP will be falling. g

Overall, national debt clearly has the potential to harm an economy. This is only really the case when the level of debt is considered unsustainable, which occurs when there is a genuine fear that the government will be unable to pay back the money owed. Given that in the UK most debt is held domestically by pension funds on a long-term basis, it can be concluded that the high level of debt is not particularly harmful, as there is no pressure for the government to pay the money back quickly and therefore no genuine fear in markets of the government defaulting. h

e **25/25 marks awarded.** a There is strong analysis throughout the answer, which begins with a recognition that high levels of debt can cause uncertainty. b The impact this could have on the economy is well explained, with brilliant analysis detailing how debt could easily spiral out of control once high levels of debt begin to affect consumer and investor confidence. c A strong explanation is offered of the inter-generational inequality that high levels of national debt can cause. d The analysis ends with a strong argument illustrating the significant opportunity cost rising debt causes the government. e The evaluation is very strong as it suggests national debt is of great concern only when it is extremely high, demonstrating using recent economic history that the current levels of debt do not fall into this category. f This is further supported by the recognition that the UK government is currently able to finance its high levels of debt because of low interest rates, which limits the negative impact such debt causes. g The student argues that, providing the economy is growing, national debt can actually be falling as a percentage of GDP even when the absolute amount of debt is rising. h An excellent supported judgement is reached which ultimately demonstrates that the nature of the UK's debt means it is not as great a concern for the economy as it might otherwise be under different circumstances.

Student B

National debt in the UK is now at nearly double the level recommended as the ceiling level of debt by the sustainable investment rule. When national debt is at such high levels, there is a danger that the interest rates charged on borrowing may increase, as lenders consider the economy riskier to lend to because of the high level of debt owed. This could make it more challenging for the government to service its debt, forcing it to raise taxes or cut spending in other areas, which could harm economic growth. a

High levels of debt could also cause the government problems when it comes to refinancing this debt. If lenders believe debt is beyond a sustainable level it may be that rather than charge a higher interest rate they simply decide that lending to the country is too risky. This could cause a crisis for the government, as they may be unable to undertake the borrowing they need to meet their spending commitments. This could lead to the government defaulting on its debt interest payments and being forced into dramatic reductions in government spending because it has essentially run out of money. The consequences of this would be deep and long lasting for the economy. b

However, national debt is not as harmful when it is clear that it is only temporary. It is understandable that debt increased significantly during the recession, as the government needed to stimulate the economy towards a recovery. Providing the debt begins to reduce as a percentage of GDP following the recession, this is unlikely to cause the problems previously discussed. Given that national debt has fluctuated as a percentage of GDP over time and has not been continually rising, this makes the level of debt more credible and therefore less problematic. c

e 13/25 marks awarded. a A good analysis is offered of the risk of rising interest rates caused by excessive national debt. b The potential chaos which could result from the government defaulting on its debt is well explained, although it must be said that this is unlikely at the level of debt outlined in the question – it is unrealistic to suggest that at current debt levels the UK government would be unable to find willing lenders, although it is reasonable to suggest this could happen if national debt continued to rise. c The evaluation is reasonable. The point that high levels of national debt are not problematic because this represents natural cyclical adjustment is technically valid but perhaps underestimates the scale of the problem currently experienced in the UK, where debt increased so dramatically and has continued to increase as a percentage of GDP many years after the economy came out of recession.

Knowledge check answers

1 A shift in the PPC from PPC_0 to PPC_1 (long-run growth) with actual output increasing from B to C (short-run growth). Here there is essentially an increase in the economy's productive capacity, which is immediately being utilised to produce more output.

2 % increase in nominal GDP = ($583bn – $537bn) ÷ $537bn × 100 = 8.57%
Real economic growth rate = 8.57% – 4.1% = **4.47%**

3 Population growth could result from an increase in the birth rate or an increase in immigration. Greater participation rates could result from reducing benefits, raising the retirement age or improving the availability of childcare.

4 Unemployment is a major cause of poverty; economic growth will increase the number of people in work to produce the higher level of output, which will take some individuals out of poverty. The government will also have more tax revenue to spend, thus improving the welfare of the poor.

5 Disabled, early retired, students over the age of 16, home-makers.

6 The ILO unemployment rate is likely to be higher than the claimant count rate because it includes individuals who are unemployed but who are either ineligible or choosing not to claim JSA.

7 Frictional unemployment suggests a degree of flexibility in the labour market. Also individuals engaging in a period of search is not necessarily a bad thing – it could mean they find a job in which they are the most productive, avoiding underemployment and therefore contributing more to GDP.

8 When unemployment benefits are high it is likely many individuals will be voluntarily unemployed because they choose not to accept low-wage jobs. There is no incentive for them to work because they believe they will be better off receiving benefits – the extra wage on offer from working is not worth sacrificing leisure time for.

9 (149 – 143) ÷ 143 × 100 = **4.20%**

10 The UK was experiencing cost-push inflation caused by rising commodity prices. The BRIC nations were experiencing demand-pull inflation caused by capacity constraints being reached, with aggregate demand rising faster than aggregate supply.

11 Average propensity to save = Saving ÷ Total income = £5,500 ÷ £30,000 = **0.18**
Average propensity to consume = 1 – Average propensity to save = 1 – 0.18 = **0.82**

12 Injections must equal leakages (i.e. Investment + Government spending + Exports = Saving + Taxes + Imports).

13 Marginal propensity to save = 1 – Marginal propensity to consume = 1 – 0.8 = 0.2
Marginal propensity to withdraw = $MPS + MPT + MPM$ = 0.2 + 0.3 + 0.1 = 0.6

Multiplier = 1 ÷ Marginal propensity to withdraw = 1 ÷ 0.6 = 1.67

14 An increase in the price level will make domestic products relatively more expensive in comparison with products produced abroad. This will cause a decrease in demand from foreign consumers and also a decrease in demand from domestic consumers, who switch to consuming more goods from abroad. This decrease in exports and increase in imports will worsen net exports and cause a contraction along the aggregate demand curve, resulting in real output falling.

15 If consumers lack confidence about the future (for example, they anticipate there is a good chance they will lose their job), consumption is likely to fall, as individuals save more for the difficult times ahead.

16 In a recession the government will be receiving less tax revenue. This may mean it is forced to cut back on spending in order to reduce the size of the budget deficit.

17 This will increase the domestic price of imported inputs, raising firms' costs of production and therefore causing short-run aggregate supply to shift to the left.

18 Long-run aggregate supply will shift to the right from $LRAS_1$ to $LRAS_2$. This reduces inflationary pressures in the economy, with the price level falling from P_1 to P_2. Economic growth will occur, with real output increasing from Y_1 to Y_2. There will be a reduction in unemployment as derived demand for labour increases – more labour is needed to produce this higher level of output.

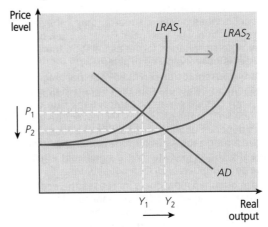

19 Proportional taxes take the same proportion of income from those on high incomes as those on low incomes. A flat tax would be an example of a proportional tax.

20 The cyclical budget position takes into account fluctuations in the government budget due to the economic cycle – you would expect there to be a cyclical deficit during times of recession, which is not a problem providing there is a cyclical surplus during boom periods. The structural budget position demonstrates the position of the government budget when the economy is at full employment – a structural deficit therefore suggests underlying problems with government finances and is therefore more damaging than a cyclical deficit.

21 As shown below, the increase in aggregate demand will generate no increase in real output as all factors of production are already fully and efficiently employed. The policy will be purely inflationary in this instance, with prices rising significantly from P_1 to P_2.

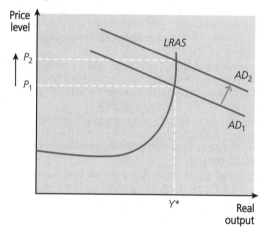

22 A symmetric inflation target means deviations below the target rate of inflation are considered equally problematic as deviations above the target rate. The UK has a symmetric target. An asymmetric target is when deviations matter only if they are in one direction. The European Central Bank has an asymmetric inflation target as inflation that is below target is not considered problematic.

23 Many households are on fixed rate mortgages, meaning the interest rate they pay on their mortgage will not change when the central bank rate changes, at least not in the short run. Moreover, the impact of this depends upon the proportion of households that have a mortgage – given home ownership is high in the UK, this is likely to have a significant effect on the consumption of British households.

24 More qualified individuals increases the economy's productive capacity only if the individuals are qualified in areas demanded by the labour market. For example, if lots of students are graduating

with degrees in History but the labour market is demanding skilled mechanics, these highly qualified graduates will not be any more skilled for the jobs on offer than they were before studying for their degree.

25 The demand for labour could decrease, increasing unemployment and worsening the standard of living for individuals who go from receiving a low wage to receiving no wage and being forced to live off benefits. Raising the minimum wage could also harm the international competitiveness of domestic firms if they are competing with firms operating in countries with lower or no minimum wage.

26 Supply-side policy, because it results in output increasing and the price level falling. Therefore, ensuring the productive capacity is increasing in line with increases in output will over time help to prevent the economy from overheating and to an extent will result in fewer policy conflicts arising.

27 The country would be reliant on other countries for many essential goods and services, which leaves it vulnerable. Moreover, if the demand for the good it produces falls then the economy would encounter a significant reduction in GDP.

28 Country C: 2 eggs; Country D: 5 eggs.

29 3,000 eggs have been traded for 1,000 t-shirts, so the terms of trade are 3 eggs for 1 t-shirt.

30 Current account balance = £21.4bn – £35.4bn – £11.8bn = –£25.8bn
= **£25.8 billion deficit**

31 It results in aggregate demand falling, meaning while the current account deficit might be corrected, it would harm the level of economic growth in the economy.

32 This will cause the supply of pounds to increase, as domestic investors get a relatively better return from saving abroad. This causes the pound to depreciate.

33 The UK government would need to purchase foreign exchange reserves, in doing so decreasing the demand for pounds/increasing the supply of pounds, which would offset any appreciation pressures.

34 This would improve the purchasing power of domestic consumers, meaning they could afford to purchase more imports and potentially increasing their standard of living. However, this comes at a cost of worsening the current account, except of course if the Marshall–Lerner condition doesn't hold, in which case there could be short-run improvements in the trade balance.